The Veil's Edge

ALSO BY WILLOW POLSON

Witch Crafts

Sabbat Entertaining

The Veil's Edge

Exploring the Boundaries of Magic

WILLOW POLSON

With a Foreword by

M. MACHA NIGHTMARE

CITADEL PRESS
Kensington Publishing Corp.
www.kensingtonbooks.com

CITADEL PRESS BOOKS are published by
Kensington Publishing Corp.
850 Third Avenue
New York, NY 10022

All Kensington titles, imprints, and distributed lines are available at special quantity discounts for bulk
purchases for sales promotions, premiums, fund-raising, educational, or institutional use. Special book
excerpts or customized printings can also be created to fit specific needs. For details, write or phone
the office of the Kensington special sales manager: Kensington Publishing Corp., 850 Third Avenue,
New York, NY 10022, attn: Special Sales Department, phone 1-800-221-2647.

Charts on pages 14, courtesy of Global Consciousness Project

First printing: April 2003

10 9 8 7 6 5 4 3 2 1

Printed in the United States of America

Library of Congress Control Number: 2002113405

ISBN 0-8065-2352-2

For the seeker of knowledge, truth, and a
better way of being, these words are my gift.

The world needs more magic—
let's bring it back together.

Contents

Foreword

By M. Macha NightMare

THERE IS A MOVEMENT AFOOT IN THE UNITED STATES, AND it's called Paganism. Paganism comes in many flavors, just as our citizenry does. The most popular form of Paganism is Witchcraft, sometimes called Wicca, although Wicca is a specific sort of Witchcraft, one that is British-based and derived primarily from the works of the late British civil servant Gerald Brousseau Gardner.

There isn't a lot of solid, irrefutable evidence of Witchcraft or Paganism having existed, at least in the forms that are now popular, prior to the 1940s. But that doesn't matter a bit. Since the 1970s and '80s, all forms of Paganism have attracted more adherents as well as having evolved in deeper and more complex ways.

Now that we have moved into the twenty-first century of the Common Era, all forms of Paganism are flourishing.

Why do I use the term *Pagan* rather than *Neo-Pagan*? What do I mean by *Pagan*? I use *Pagan* rather than *Neo-Pagan* because to use *Neo-Pagan* would imply that there was such a thing as Paleo-

Paganism or Meso-Paganism, which there wasn't. There were many belief systems and modes of practice, worship, celebration, and magic that might today be considered Pagan, but they were fragmented and isolated. Widespread, but not cohesive. By Pagan, I mean a practitioner of an Earth-based spirituality, a nature religion, or an ethnic reconstruction religion.

Evidence of this flourishing of all forms of Paganism today can be found in the plethora of new books whose authors take us deeper into the mysteries of these magical paths. Others take us deeper into the sociopolitical Pagan world. This book is one of the former.

Some authors approach magic from a scientific perspective. Willow Polson takes a broad look at recent scientific theories and how they affirm much magical thinking.

One of Paganism's primary attractions to seekers is its reverence for nature and its concern for the environment and the continued viability of our planet Earth. Science is humankind's attempt to observe and analyze Nature and natural phenonema, to understand this glorious world in which we all live and upon which we are are dependent for our very existence. Paganism has no quarrel with science. The Pagan paths and scientific inquiry have never been in opposition. The more we learn from science, the more our Pagan beliefs and practices are reinforced by science. There are some magical ways of thinking and perceiving the world that do not fit into scientific constructs, but those that do are affirmed by the hard sciences.

Nowhere is this realization more acute than in the realm of prayer, or continued human attention, both mental and emotional, to achieving a particular outcome. The efficacy of prayer, no matter who is praying to whom, has been amply demonstrated. Requests for prayers frequently go out on the Internet, via Belief-Net and other venues, whence they are widely circulated. Recipients of the "energy" directed through prayer attest to its benefits. Further, scientific studies of people undergoing risky surgery, for instance, or suffering from serious illnesses, substantiate that those for whom concerted and numerous prayers are offered, no matter the kind of prayer, recover more quickly and thoroughly than those to whom no spiritual attention is directed. I maintain that spellwork is a form of prayer; usually spellwork is accompanied and reinforced by prayer.

The same is true, I believe, of other entities such as deities. They can emerge and grow stronger when they are "fed" with prayers and other manner of attention.

An instance of scientific discovery coming into alignment with ancient magical principles is in the case of quantum mechanics. Another can be found in James Lovelock's "Gaia Hypothesis," wherein he makes a case for the Earth's being a single complex, interrelated organism. Pagans have long been aware of our interconnectedness with all of the earth's species and processes, and of our mutual interdependence.

What is "reality"? Is it an illusion? I don't believe so. I have found reality to be relative. It depends on who is perceiving and how that person is perceiving. What senses he is using, whether sight, sound, smell, taste, touch, and/or intuition. And from what perspective she views something.

The concerns with science—how things work and why—when

complemented with questions of what reality might be lead us to the liminal realms where the world of matter and the world of spirit meet. Many describe this liminal realm as being a veil, a wispy, translucent, diaphanous fabric, through which the living pass and depart the world of matter, and from which the world of spirit is made manifest.

Using one or more of several tried-and-true methods, humans seek to pierce this veil that separates the worlds of matter and spirit. They seek ecstasy. Ecstasy means to be out of the stasis, out of the normal, out of yourself. The sacred technologies that facilitate ecstatic states of consciousness and the ability to perceive other realities, other worlds, are breathwork, dance, rhythm, chant, fast, sensual stimulation, and the use of psychotropics. Commonly, Pagans seek knowledge of other worlds using these shamanic techniques. While other cultures, ancient and modern, provide a cultural context for the magic worker to operate, Pagans today are relearning and/or creating communities and environments and mutual support for these technicians of the sacred.

Pagans re-create the sacred rites of the sweat lodge, the sauna, and other purifications. They erect stone circles, build cairns, and walk labyrinths. Modern practitioners do these things in ways adapted to the circumstances—mostly urban and suburban—of our modern lives.

Witches and other Pagans form study groups. They find one another and begin small working groups. They search and experiment and give each other feedback. They research deities ancient and modern, and allow their remembered voices to be heard again. This concerted work creates deep bonds among those who share

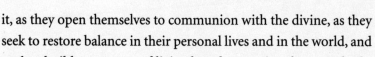

it, as they open themselves to communion with the divine, as they seek to restore balance in their personal lives and in the world, and as they build a new way of living based on ancient lore, methods, and connection.

Each author who looks afresh and deeper at the many symbols and systems that go into making contemporary Pagan practices adds to our culture. Each book is a building block. Let us read them with pleasure and discernment.

—San Rafael, California
September 2002

Preface

I WAS TALKING TO A FRIEND ABOUT MAGIC BEFORE I STARTED writing this book. She used to consider herself a Witch years ago, but stopped acting on her beliefs because she couldn't find a coven to work with and the books at the time—the late 1970s—were little more than personal memoirs or medieval grimoires (and bad grimoires at that).

In expressing interest in getting back into Witchcraft, she said in frustration, "I know that magic is supposed to work, but I need proof. The logical part of my brain just can't get around the idea that magic makes no sense and shouldn't work."

Many people, in this age of science and reason, really do need proof that magic works. It is to you folks with an analytical and perhaps skeptical mind that the first two chapters of this book are dedicated. Look no further for proof that magic not only exists, but that it works and can affect our daily reality as much as we want it to. From quantum physics to medical experiments and shamanism, I will give you documented examples of how people are using magic to change the world.

Building on that solid base of proof, I've taken some ideas to their logical conclusions and taken others on wild, unexplored tangents. I've related some of my own experiences and contacted Pagan elders for their viewpoints on this thing called magic. We owe it to ourselves and our world to try to find new ways, deeper ways, to communicate with the divine and shape our realities.

In recent years, some of my friends and temple kin have complained that there's a flood of "newbie" Pagan books on the shelves, but nothing really "advanced" for experienced practitioners to sink their teeth into. This complaint seems to be borne out by a survey on The Witches' Voice (www.witchvox.com), which asked what people wanted to see in Pagan books; the answer was overwhelmingly "not another Wicca 101."

I hope that this book is not viewed as "another Wicca 101," since I did my best to explore the boundaries of magic and workings that people are doing right now. Some of the information presented here may seem shocking, or ridiculous, or impossible, but that's what pushing the envelope is about. Somewhere between the "what if" and the "wow" is where you ought to be—not simply a passenger, but one of the people driving the bus and exploring new territories to bring more magic back to the world.

Naturally, without the right training and perhaps help from others, some of the ideas and techniques in this book could be somewhat dangerous. No, there aren't any recipes for explosives or spells to harm others, but you could accidentally harm yourself and those around you if you get in over your head or use some of these techniques in a destructive way. If you'd like to maintain your sanity and safety, be absolutely sure you are capable of working with some of these magics, and at the very least work with experienced partners you trust if you have any hesitation about some of these workings.

Some of these techniques and magics go well outside basic Wicca 101 training, and, truth be told, outside Wicca altogether. There are Faerie magics that, if you are not compatible with them, may do any number of the things you hear about in stories, which are rarely beneficial to you (remember Rip Van Winkle?). The book also discusses things such as deep shamanism, which should only be undertaken by those experienced with trance, and allowing yourself to be "ridden" by spirits and deities.

Obviously, these things are nothing to be playing around with, especially if you don't have much experience with very deep trancing, psychic self-defense, intense group work, and other more complicated techniques. I hate to use the term *advanced,* since to some practitioners these techniques may come naturally. But for most, only years of experience and guidance from elders will enable you to practice these techniques safely and with beneficial results. By all means, explore them as far as you feel safe doing so, but don't push yourself if you're not ready.

Some people will scoff and say, "There's nothing hard in this book! I learned all this stuff in my First Degree training," or something similar. To them I say, "Hurrah! Good for you. You don't need this book, then." To all my other readers, I give you this gift of new ideas and the experiences of others who have been there to help you further your work.

A little bit about what this book is not: It is not a manual of magic that holds your hand and tells you how to do things in five easy steps. It is not intended for people with little or no training in magic workings. It is not a compendium of everything being done and explored in the magical world. It is not a platform for me to blather about "this is the only real true way" or other similar nonsense. It is not based on any one path, faith, belief system, or religion.

A little bit about what this book is: It is a jumping-off place for you to make your own discoveries. It is a resource for experienced and skillful magic workers. It is a good cross section of some of the types of things being done by people all over the world at the moment. It is for anyone seeking to expand her understanding of her own faith, especially traditions that use magic workings and direct deity contact as part of worship.

Flexibility and expanded knowledge are vital to practitioners who, as they fall into the "Elder" category more and more, will be asked to help with particularly difficult workings or may find themselves in the middle of a magical mess that only they (and perhaps their coven or group) will have the experience and power to clean up properly. This book is a springboard for learning some of those unfamiliar areas that may crop up, and for finding out how to discover more about them. I invite anyone who discovers something new and amazing after having read this book, or after having an adventure of her own not covered here in these pages, to write to me and let me know what happened—I enjoy a good story as much as anyone, and I may include it in future revisions (with permission, of course). A day without learning something new is like a day without sunshine . . . or something like that.

We may be small parts of a larger whole, people who feel insignificant when gazing at the night sky, but we can look outward

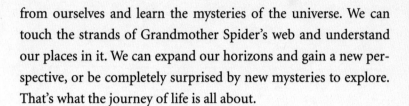

from ourselves and learn the mysteries of the universe. We can touch the strands of Grandmother Spider's web and understand our places in it. We can expand our horizons and gain a new perspective, or be completely surprised by new mysteries to explore. That's what the journey of life is all about.

Acknowledgments

AS ALWAYS, THIS BOOK WOULD NOT HAVE BEEN POSSIBLE IF not for the help of my dear soul mate and husband, Craig. I also owe a lot to my wonderful editor Margaret Wolf, who helped me tremendously through the whole thing (especially during deadline hell!) and who has a wickedly fun sense of humor. Of course I must mention my two terrific caregivers who helped to watch my son so I could work, Grandma Laney and Kathi. I also want to thank all the great people who have written to me with praise and words of encouragement, especially all my Internet friends and Web site visitors around the world. Thanks also to my dear sister-friend Denise who kept my spirits up in hard times, and to my new friend M. Macha NightMare for all the information, commiseration, and virtual hugs. A big thank-you to everyone who helped me create this book, including all the terrific folks who filled out lengthy questionnaires or who just answered a few vital questions for me. Thanks to Hayao Miyazaki and the Wachowski brothers for having Vision and keeping true to it. Priase to Hodwy, Dog of Lysdexia. And finally, nothing in my life would be as good without

the amazing energy of the deities who watch over me and have gifted me in so many ways—praise to all the Netjeru and the Old Ones.

All your base are belong to us . . .

The Veil's Edge

1

The Science Behind the Magic

"If you think you understand [quantum mechanics], that only shows you don't know the first thing about it."   —NIELS BOHR

"What we observe is not nature itself, but nature exposed to our method of questioning."
                    —WERNER HEISENBERG

"It seems to me that the least you can say is that we were wrong to think that Nature goes her merry way and we just look at Her. That is wrong. Someday someone is going to find a way to ask questions of Nature and the answers She gives back are going to blow us away. I hope I'm around when that happens."   —NICK HERBERT

THE TASTE OF A PERFECTLY RIPE STRAWBERRY. THE SCENT OF a lover's skin. The texture of a kitten's fur. The sight of a brilliant butterfly's wing. The sound of a drumbeat that speaks to your very soul.

We acknowledge that the material world affects our mind, so why are scientists having such a hard time accepting that the mind affects the material world? Physical activity releases endorphins, which better our mood. Different pieces of music can be described through emotion, like "sad" or "happy." Most health-care plans have already begun to pay for "alternative" medical therapies such as acupuncture and biofeedback. And what about the placebo effect? It's been known for years that simply thinking that a treatment will help *does* help—scientific experiments even take this effect into account when analyzing the test results.

No matter how much some scientists would like to think of mind and matter as two completely opposed concepts, the gap between them is much more of a friendly gray area than a hopeless, unbridgeable chasm. In addition, living creatures (such as ourselves) are not mindless automatons without free will, and the same is true of the components of the rest of the universe, whether looking at the outward cosmic scale or the inward microscopic scale. Through years of experimentation, scientists have come to the conclusion (but not without kicking and screaming and gnashing of teeth) that the world is much more random than Sir Isaac Newton and other "clockwork universe" scientists ever could have guessed.

Before the current quantum theories emerged and flowered in the twentieth century, Newtonian physics used a mechanical model of how everything worked. Cause and effect of objects on each other were all that could be understood before the invention of sophisticated equipment to measure subatomic particles, so it was believed that everything operated under constant, immovable laws of nature—like a clockwork automaton.

Beginning in the late nineteenth century, however, scientists ran into things that could not be explained by the traditional mechanical model. Light particles didn't behave the way scientists thought they should, light waves were just as mysterious in their actions, the results of exacting experiments sometimes didn't turn out exactly the same when repeated, and, perhaps the catalyst of it all, new methods of investigating subatomic particles came into being and allowed scientists to more fully measure and understand the actions of atoms and pieces of atoms on each other. New ideas had to be explored, and quantum indeterminism was put forth as a theory. In it, the clockwork universe is dead—rather than everything simply being true or false, off or on, all matter operates within a range of possible outcomes. Traditional physics was turned on its head, and traditional scientists didn't like it a bit.

Albert Einstein, one of the greatest thinkers of our time, responded to the theory of quantum indeterminism with the angry claim that "God does not play dice with the universe!" But as much as he wished that to be true—and he spent the rest of his life trying to prove the existence of a clockwork universe—his wish was not fulfilled. Science has proven the theory that every action of every atomic particle is based on chance and probability. On top of that, the more these probabilities are investigated, the stranger the universe appears to the human mind. To quote Stephen Hawking, "God not only plays dice, He also sometimes throws the dice where they cannot be seen."

True, it is not the sort of chance that changes physical reality completely on a moment-by-moment basis (that we are aware of), but it is enough to make the action of each particle not quite as predictable as Einstein would have liked. In fact, it appears that simply observing the workings and/or results of an experiment irrevocably changes the experiment and/or results.

A popular example put forth by Nobel physicist Erwin Schrödinger is that of Schrödinger's cat. In this theoretical experiment that the popular cartoonist and inventor of ridiculous mechanisms Rube Goldberg would be proud of, a subatomic particle is contained in a small box with a detector and counter mechanism. When (or if) a counter registers that the particle has decayed, a hammer crashes down onto a glass bottle filled with cyanide, and a cat contained in a box with the cyanide is instantly killed.

The paradox is this: Schrödinger claims that the fate of the cat is not determined until it is observed, leaving the unfortunate cat in the state of being both dead and alive until someone opens the box to see what happened. It can be argued that the cat knows whether it's dead or not, and the experiment was "observed" by the monitor and counter, leaving any human contact out of it and making the result predetermined before we ever opened the box. But this example is flawed since it deals in the macroworld with a sentient cat—it evolved to help explain what may be happening in the invisible microworld of individual atoms and particles when an action is measured.

A better example of the possibilities that quantum science offers may be the Copenhagen Interpretation formulated by Niels Bohr (who did much of his work in Copenhagen). Reportedly,

Bohr replied to Einstein's view of God's unwillingness to gamble by tossing back "Don't tell God what to do!" Perhaps Ian Stewart put it best in his book *Does God Play Dice?* when he said:

> Perhaps God can play dice, and create a universe of complete law and order, in the same breath. The question is not so much *whether* God plays dice, but *how* God plays dice.

So instead of looking at chaos as being devoid of a divine or cosmic "plan," if you will, perhaps we should instead understand that it *is* the plan. Or perhaps chaos and the clockwork universe actually coexist quite happily, even if we humans have trouble measuring or understanding that.

Bohr's idea took the concept of the observer affecting the experiment to its logical conclusion: Everything we perceive, or measure by observation, isn't real until it is observed. Now, this naturally goes against everything we understand about the laws of nature and would seem to put human interaction at the top of some chain of measurement. That is part of the problem—at what point in the chain does the measurement occur and determine reality? Does Schrödinger's cat constitute an observer? Does a sentient deity? Does the flea on the cat's back? No one really knows.

A recent (1998) experiment by researchers at the Weizman Institute of Science proved the Uncertainty Principle theory of Werner Karl Heismann, which states that measuring the movement of particles alters their actions, and that a particle can only be described in terms of probabilities, since we can never truly know what the action of the particle might have been had we not been measuring it. The experimenters created a tiny "observer," which was able to detect the movements of electrons by using an electric charge. The more the "observer" mechanism "watched" the electrons, the more electrical current ran through it, and the more this altered the flow of the electrons it was "watching."

When I first read about this study, I figured that an electric charge would certainly alter something as tiny as electrons and the study was flawed. But as the following interchange between Dr. Jeffrey Mishlove and Dr. Fred Alan Wolf on the PBS television series *Thinking Allowed* shows, simply looking at something or being conscious of it affects the outcome of a particle's actions:

> WOLF: In ordinary physics... perception is something which is taken to be outside the realm of physicality. In other words, if you perceive something, you know that you see something. Light will strike your retina; you'll get an idea, or something will pop off in your brain, or something of that sort. But we never got the notion that somehow the act of seeing something was affecting what you were seeing or looking at. But in quantum physics we've learned that when you're looking at very small objects, subatomic particles for example, the very action of looking at them disturbs them to such an extent that we never really get a complete picture as to what they actually are. Now, this has led me to think that consciousness may be at the core of this problem as to how perception can affect and change reality, and that maybe what we're doing when we're thinking or feeling or sensing or even listening to a

conversation is using this action of consciousness, this fundamental act...that suddenly alters the physical reality of, say, the human body.

MISHLOVE: In other words, in subatomic physics, if I want to look at a particle, I literally have to touch it. I have to bounce a photon or something off of it in order to do that. What you're suggesting is that consciousness acts in this way; it touches the things that it perceives.

WOLF: That's right.

MISHLOVE: It almost becomes one with them, merges with them a little bit, in the process of perceiving.

WOLF: Right. The way I kind of look at it is that consciousness is a huge oceanic wave that washes through everything, and it has ripples and vibrations in it. When there are acts of consciousness, the wave turns into bubbles at that moment, it just turns into froth...I think this action takes place not only in our minds and our brains, but even at the level of the subatomic particles that make us up. In fact, that may be how the universe got created in the first place.

Obviously, this line of thinking can be paralleled directly with a lot of creation stories from around the world. In many traditions, the Supreme Being simply existed in the vast chaos of space (or the ocean, or the darkness, or what have you) and became a consciousness that began to create the order of the universe and separate dualities, eventually creating the Earth as we know it.

We live in a very exciting time—physicists are beginning to realize that thought affects the physical world and explore the ideas of alternate realities as science fact rather than science fiction. They're seeing that the universe is incredibly strange to the human mind, and the more they explore it, the stranger it shows itself to be. For so long science and religion have been at odds, but when you have renowned scientists in the field of quantum physics coming up with theories that the universe began with a conscious thought, well, that's a happy marriage indeed, in my opinion. It seems like something's come full circle, or full spiral in any event, since the ancients came to the same conclusion through very different methods.

But what does all this have to do with magic? Knowing that all actions of atomic matter are based on degrees of probability, rather than a mechanical clockwork universe, and taking the Uncertainty Principle into account, we realize that *we can affect anything simply by being aware of it.*

Every time you do anything magical, or even think about something with any intensity at all, you have looked into Schrödinger's box and altered the outcome. You can wish for a positive outcome for that job interview, which can alter the probability of it slightly, but we're talking about affecting things on a subatomic level of energy. A big ol' wonkin' spell to get you that job, however, is going to affect probability a large amount and increase your chances dramatically. This is how and why magic works—you are affecting the probability, or likelihood, of an event occurring (or not occurring).

I also believe that this is part of how divinity works. If an entity is "fed" with energy, prayers, attention, even fear, it becomes stronger and has more power to influence the world. Even people who have become saints or deities receive this same kind of energy in the afterlife and thus have the divine power to change things. For example, a forgotten god from thousands of years ago may not have much (or any) power or influence, but a popular goddess who receives praise daily and is often called on for help can perform miracles. That's why I think it's pretty darn funny that some Christians are so freaked out about Satan, when they're the ones feeding him energy! If they'd just stop getting into a lather and turn their backs on him, perhaps declaring "you have no power here," he would be a lot less of a threat to them.

Back to the issue at hand. "Okay," you might say, "but aren't we talking about matter versus magic? Subatomic particles are still made of 'stuff,' and thought isn't 'stuff,' right?" Yes and no—particles are primarily energy, as our brain waves are—and particles make up all the matter we experience on a daily basis. So your thoughts are every bit as real as the chair you're sitting in, and similarly measurable, now that we've invented the increasingly sensitive equipment to read brain waves.

In a University of Pennsylvania study, scientists used a brain imaging technique to study what goes on in the mind of a Tibetan Buddhist monk as he reaches a "transcendental high." Dr. Andrew Newberg and his team compared the scans of meditating monks and the same monks when they are in a normal waking state.

"There was an increase in activity in the front part of the brain, the area that is activated when anyone focuses attention on a particular task," said Dr. Newberg, and he went on to describe how the parts of the brain that influence spatial awareness and orientation have a dramatic decrease in activity during deep meditation. "During meditation, people have a loss of the sense of self and frequently experience a sense of no space and time and that was exactly what we saw," he said. Similar results were found in an earlier study of the "centering" prayers of Franciscan nuns.

More important than these bare facts, however, is that the study proves the existence of a dramatic change in brain activity and function during deep meditation. Perceptions are different from those in a resting or waking state, and a scientifically measurable inner shift takes place. It may be "all in the mind," but instead of meaning that what the meditating person experiences isn't real, the phrase now describes a very real inner landscape that can be accessed by anyone who knows how to reach a deep meditative state.

Dr. Newberg went on to say, "When someone has a mystical experience, they perceive that sense of reality to be far greater and far clearer than our usual everyday sense of reality. Since the sense of spiritual reality is more powerful and clear, perhaps that sense of reality is more accurate than our scientific everyday sense of reality."

Basing his research on that of the late Eugene d'Aquili, Dr. Newberg has developed a biological theory of religion, which ties human physiology and brain function to what appears to be a basic need for religion. But rather than using science to explain away the divine, he sees his research as reinforcing the reality of the divine. In an interview that recently appeared in *Reader's Digest,* Dr.

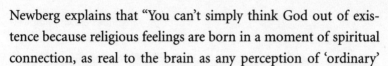

Newberg explains that "You can't simply think God out of existence because religious feelings are born in a moment of spiritual
connection, as real to the brain as any perception of 'ordinary'
physical reality."

Author of the article Vince Rause asks in return, "Does this
mean that God is just a perception generated by the brain, or has
the brain been wired to experience the reality of God?"

"The best and most rational answer I can give to both questions
is yes," replies Dr. Newberg. "Reality is a matter of degree—what
feels most real *is* most real."

As Rause puts it so beautifully in his article:

> Mystical experience, I was beginning to understand, was a
> quiet, personal epiphany that the miraculous and the mun-
> dane are one and the same, and that both are right before
> our eyes. Soon I learned that, for the mystics, it is only when
> the self is pushed aside during meditation that we can see re-
> ality as it truly is.

Once again we intertwine the ideas of science and what could
be called magic, divinity, or any number of other religious and
spiritual concepts. If the state of meditation is measurable, and we
know that the parts of the brain dealing with orientation, relax-
ation, time and space, and reasoning are all affected by meditation,
which reality is more real? And what if we desire to change reality
with concentrated thought? With magic?

Another experiment related to the concept of the human mind

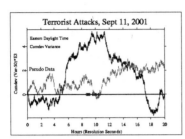

This graph shows the dramatic difference between expected randomness in the "eggs" (pseudodata) and the actual variance from randomness on September 11, 2001. There is an indication that the effects registered for this horrendous event might have begun several hours prior to the first attack.

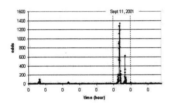

This figure shows the 2-tailed probabilities associated with the smoothed Z-score as odds ratios. There is an extraordinary spike near the time of the attacks, driven by large deviations that precede the first plane crashing into the World Trade Center towers; its weighted center is at 06:10, corresponding to the peak in the Z scores. The second spike occurs roughly seven hours later, with the weighted center at about 1:00 P.M.

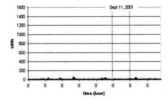

To help assure that there was no mistake in the processing, this same figure was recreated using algorithmically generated pseudo-random data instead of the real data generated by the truly random eggs located in countries all around the world. This figure speaks for itself.

affecting the physical world is the Global Consciousness Project (GCP) being researched by Princeton University in New Jersey. The GCP has placed "eggs" containing computers that generate random numbers all over the world—and the results have been startling. When large numbers of people all pay attention to the same thing, such as a disaster or day of world prayer, the numbers being generated become slightly less random to varying degrees. For example, the World Trade Center disaster in September 2001 created a large spike of reduced randomness in the eggs.

This experiment, which is ongoing, proves that human attention concentrated on an event alters physical reality. Computers that are simply generating random numbers in their processors have been affected by the minds of human beings and produce a different outcome. If that isn't proof that magic works, I don't know what is.

There are those who refuse to acknowledge that this is possible, even in the face of what seems like such overwhelming evidence. Alastair Rae, in his book *Quantum Physics: Illusion or Reality?* goes 99 percent of the way toward accepting this idea but then stops at the door:

> . . . if the cat is both alive and dead until someone looks at it, then mind is apparently influencing matter. Are we then in a position to explain psychokinesis in which some conscious minds with particular powers are said to be able to cause objects to move around rooms or to bend spoons or whatever? . . . Even if the mind is the final (or the only) measuring apparatus, *it acts as a measuring apparatus*. . . . This

> influence is limited to determining the nature of the possible outcomes of the experiment...and therefore cannot affect the...results.

Rae's mistake is in assuming that the mind has no influence outside of the function of measurement. However, as magic workers we know that our energies can indeed influence outside events, and science again backs this up in the form of studies regarding prayer.

In a 2001 study, Duke University researchers found that postoperative complications related to coronary artery surgery were reduced by up to 30 percent in the group that was prayed for versus the control group that was not. Information about the patients was sent to various prayer groups around the world, and included Buddhists, Jews, and various Christian sects, which all sent the patients healing energies and prayed for their health and recovery. Other studies show that when a patient is part of a prayer group, they do far better, and there are dramatic stories of patients who are near death making "miraculous" recoveries and going on to live normal lives after having participated in these groups.

This phenomenon of remote prayer groups affecting patients in hospitals many miles away, often called "distant healing," has been the object of some studies by Dr. Elisabeth Targ, who has been interested in its possibilities since the 1960s. In perhaps one of her best-known studies, from 1998, Dr. Targ and other researchers conducted a double-blind study on AIDS patients in San Francisco. Two groups were selected and controlled for other factors,

then one had distant healing efforts directed at it while the control group received none. The group receiving the distant healing reported significantly fewer AIDS-related illnesses and doctor visits, as well as less severe symptoms and an improvement in mood.

According to the peer commentary of this study from *Journal Watch*:

> This is an interesting result in a well-designed study in which the differences in outcome are not likely to be explained by the placebo effect. In fact, we have no explanation of how this effect occurred.

I think readers of this book, however, have some inkling as to how this may have occurred.

The question remains, however: Why is it that some scientists are so eager to dismiss things they cannot measure? If you take your car before a group of experts, the engineer will comment on how it is constructed or the engine's horsepower, the artist will admire its aesthetics, the environmentalist will lament its poor gas mileage, and the dealer will tell you how much it's worth in its current condition. None of them is wrong, but they are all measuring separate things while ignoring the rest of the car's features.

As well, societal experts gnash their teeth over the rate of teen crime or fatherless children, but fail to find reasons behind why these things occur. All the while, traditional scientists from their pedestals wave away any notion of how the spirit world can possibly affect the lives of the masses. Their God is made up of mathematical equations and laboratory experiments. "We cannot measure things like Reiki or magic or faeries," they scoff, "so thus they are not real."

So from our previous example of the car, does the artist refuse to believe in the existence of the car's brakes? Or does the engineer dismiss the notion of upholstery? Certainly not—both are simply measuring something else. The entire car is still there, just as magic is still there. Scientists are simply using equipment that is unable to measure magic, or they're pointing their microscopes at the wrong thing.

I certainly don't mean to paint all scientists with a broad brush— many scientists are devoutly spiritual. It's the ones who look down their noses at the rest of us for believing that magic works and that what has been categorized as "impossible" is indeed possible that I have a problem with. Just as Newton, the originator of the idea of a clockwork universe, would probably have thought that quantum physics was a load of nonsense, there are those today who think magic is a load of nonsense. And frankly, I think that shows a lack of imagination and lack of faith in something larger than what they can personally measure—something that I think starts slipping into overconfidence in one's abilities and perhaps even arrogance.

In another example of the ability of humans to heal through mental ability alone, biophysicist Dr. Beverly Rubik of San Francisco State University conducted experiments involving the psychic "healing" of bacteria samples. In this excerpt from the *Thinking Allowed* series, she describes this work:

RUBIK: Well, the research stemmed from my dissertation work, of course. I'd spent some six or seven years studying bacterial growth and motility...

MISHLOVE: Motility means their ability to move around.

RUBIK: Right...and so I was well versed in that system; it wasn't like I pulled it out of thin air and subjected people to study it. But I was very familiar with it, and I knew when in fact I intoxicated my bacteria with a certain dose of a certain chemical agent, that indeed they would not swim. And what we found with some of the psychic healers such as Dr. Olga Worral...is that she was seemingly able to revive a certain percentage of them. We found about seven percent motility in that experiment, as I recall.

MISHLOVE: Where you would expect none.

RUBIK: Where we saw virtually none. I've done that over and over again as a control experiment—many, many times over six or seven years—in the course of my dissertation work.

MISHLOVE: I think that research stands as a model, in terms of what the scientific method is capable of accomplishing as we look at parapsychological phenomena, and it's probably very important in the history of science itself, and the convergence of science and spirituality.

This set of experiments is not only important on its own, but also adds to the mounting evidence that the human mind and spirit can affect the world in dramatic ways.

So far we have seen scientifically proven examples of distant healing and revival of bacteria. Sandra Ingerman is not a scientist-turned-believer but rather a shaman turning to science to validate her experiments with water. In them, Ingerman starts with deionized water with a pH of 5.5, and pours it into two bowls. The control bowl is left untouched and placed in another room. To the experimental bowl is added two droppers of ammonium hydroxide, resulting in a pH of 11.5 and thus making the water unsafe to drink.

Next, Ingerman and three other women do an extensive shamanic healing of the water in sacred space, using visualization, chants, music, and prayers. The water in the experimental bowl in one example was changed to a pH of 9, making it safely drinkable, while the control bowl remained at 11.5 as verified by an independent lab test. In other repeated experiments, some over many miles and with participants in different locations, the pH changed from 12 to 9, 11 to 9.5, 11 to 10, and 11.5 to 10.

Ingerman's work, done from the perspective of a shaman rather than a scientist, goes far in proving yet again that the human mind affects material reality in a measurable way in a repeatable scientific study. It would be interesting to see this experiment performed in a professional laboratory setting—would the results be less or more dramatic? Because the experiments are ongoing, perhaps we will see this happen in the near future.

In all of the examples given thus far, people from many different traditions have used only their minds to exact changes to the "real" world. It appears that most of them have used a special connection to what they consider the Supreme Being or Creator and channeled this power to a person, entity, or substance so that it could be transmuted according to the worker's wishes. I don't know if any of them have worked with the idea of stepping outside reality, a concept discussed in the next chapter.

Opening up a channel to the Source appears to be how many healers do their work, from shamanic healing to Reiki, prayer circles to Wiccan covens. But science, usually considered devoid of any recognition of a greater power, also shows us methods by which we can heal, and influence, and change, and shape.

Ultimate objectivity being the goal, scientific study does not generally allow the idea of an outside influence causing change, even in the face of quantum theory. It appears to depend on the scientific community's comfort level with the divine, with some scientists rejecting any notion that "God" could be causing experiments to come out differently each time, and others attributing the creation of the world and everything in it to this divine outside influence. Obviously, this is a huge gray area, and I present it as something for you to ponder—it is much too large a debate for the scope of this book.

The point of this chapter is to show, through many avenues of scientific proof, that the human mind can have a dramatic influence on the world around us. There are surely many other studies that are not covered here, as well as ideas and techniques of manipulating what we consider "reality," some of which will be dealt with in later chapters. I believe this collection of studies and experiments, however, gives a clear picture that magic is indeed real, and that every one of us can use our influence to nudge the cosmic dice and change the outcome of an event or timeline. Knowledge is power—use it well.

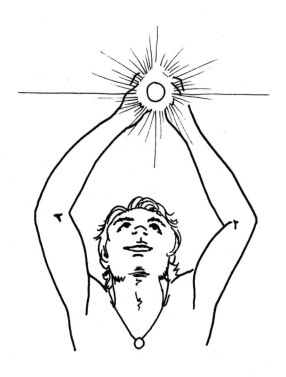

2

Reality Is an Illusion

"The only existing things are atoms and empty space—all else is mere opinion."
—DEMOCRITUS OF ABDERA

"Everything we call real is made of things that cannot be regarded as real." —NIELS BOHR

"Men have called me mad, but the question is not yet settled, whether madness is or is not the loftiest intelligence, whether much that is glorious, whether all that is profound, does not spring from disease of thought, from moods of mind exalted at the expense of the general intellect."
—EDGAR ALLAN POE

"Do not try to bend the spoon—that's impossible. Instead, only try to realize the truth . . . there is no spoon." —THE MATRIX

IMAGINE WHAT LIFE WOULD BE LIKE IF YOU COULD CREATE everything you see by imagining it to be so. Would you be lost and disoriented, not knowing where to begin or what to create? Would you go on a spree and turn plants red, double the size of your cat, and enable yourself to fly? Would you become fearful of how your actions would affect everyone else?

As we saw in the last chapter, we can influence the world around us simply by being aware we can and using belief and/or magic to change things. Knowing that, I'm about to show you how you can alter "reality" more than you ever dreamed possible.

Perhaps you've seen the film *The Matrix*. Aside from being terrific entertainment (and my favorite movie ever), this amazing film develops the concept that "reality is not what you may think." In fact, it's probably one of the most mainstream ways this idea has entered the public psyche in recent years.

In the film, the main character Neo is forced to realize that everything he thought was real is only an illusion. The truly real world of the film is only a rude awakening into a nightmare. But once he understands this and allows himself to see the illusion for what it is, he can control it like a dream reality and do the impossible. So in the end, the Matrix is still an illusion, but there's enough flesh on the bones that it can still be manipulated into another kind of reality.

What we usually think of as reality works the same way. As previously discussed, your will and your magic are capable of enacting real change in the real world. You send energy to someone who's ill and he recovers faster. You focus on a world event and the results can be measured. But what is the real world?

When you see a green leaf, you and virtually everyone around you will agree that the leaf is green. Perhaps you learned this as a small child who tried to color the leaves on the page purple, but were corrected by a parent who handed you a green crayon and suggested you color them "like real leaves." But the leaf is not green and never was.

Everything you see through your eyes is the result of light bouncing off an object and getting routed to your brain, where you filter the information and come to a conclusion about it. But what light is left behind on the object? Everything you don't see. The "green" leaf absorbs all the other colors, bouncing off the only color that it does not absorb—green. For convenience sake, we say the leaf is green, and all agree to that in our consensual reality to make things go smoother, just like we say the sun comes up and goes down when the sun is actually stationary. So it's pretty ironic that green is the only color the leaf isn't.

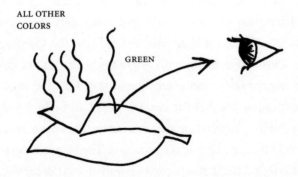

ALL OTHER COLORS

GREEN

The "green" leaf absorbs all colors of light except green, which is reflected to the eye and gives the illusion that the leaf is green.

On top of that little mind twister, you have to remember that perceptions differ in each person. Circumstances, physical differences in how we see, past experience, and probably a hundred other factors all contribute to how a person sees, understands, and experiences a situation.

Consider the example of crime witnesses. If fifteen people see a speeding car that causes an accident, you'll get fifteen different reports about what exactly happened. This is magnified by time—the longer the time elapsed since the accident, the more different or distorted the reports become. Law enforcement officials understand this and take it into account, trying to get as many witnesses as possible to cross-check the facts and questioning them carefully as soon after the event as possible. But if fifteen different people see the exact same event, why don't they all remember it exactly the same way?

The human mind may be an amazing computer, but it's not perfect and relies on its operator to process data. All people have mental filters, memories, preconceptions, and things they've learned that interfere with the pure signal that enters their senses. So the classic car collector may have noticed that the speeding car was a black 1970 Ford Shelby with original wheels, but not given the driver any consideration at all. The little old lady trying to cross the street might say that the car was going a hundred miles an hour but not have noticed anything about the car or the driver in her efforts to escape a Deathrace 2000 fate. The Hawaiian man may have noticed that the driver looked Hawaiian and the car was dark with a lei hanging from the rearview mirror, but nothing else.

Obviously, the observers noticed what was important or interesting to them personally first; any other information pretty much fell by the wayside. This is part of how consensual reality works—we can cross-reference with each other to get a larger overall picture of an event or thing, but when it comes to zooming in for the details, the results are generally rather flawed.

In another example of how individuals experience reality differently, there is a condition called synesthesia that somehow combines different types of sensory brain waves into one. People with this condition see certain letters in color, taste shapes, or experience sound in a visual way. For centuries it was thought that this genetic condition was merely "all in the head" or the work of fakes, but recent research has proven that synesthesia is real and appears to be most common among talented and gifted people such as composers, poets, artists, and scientists. It's unknown how many synesthetes there are, but estimates range from one in three hundred to one in several thousand.

All of this information brings us to a very important point. As science writer Lee Dye points out in his recent article about synesthesia:

> What, after all, is real? Green numbers are green because they occupy that specific region of the color spectrum. If someone sees a number that is painted in green, and perceives it as blue, is he seeing the real world?

That is the kernel at the center of the idea of "consensual reality." The sky is blue because we all agree that it is. But what about the color-blind person? If he sees a red sky, does he think "I'm seeing the color blue," or does he think to himself "I see a red sky... I wonder what a blue sky would look like?" His perception of the sky is his own personal reality apart from most other people who do see a blue sky.

But who can say whether any of us sees a blue sky? Perhaps when I look out my office window and see the sky as blue, I'm seeing a different color, having learned that whatever the color is it's called blue, and I'm actually seeing something different than what everyone else sees. Perhaps that's what you see, too. But in my daily life I look at the sky, see the color blue, and go about my business because it really doesn't matter. My mundane daily reality is not affected because I'm agreeing to the consensual reality that the sky is blue.

But what if I choose not to go along with consensual reality?

As discussed in the previous chapter, we know that intent can alter the outcome of an event or timeline. You cast a spell to help get a job and three offers fall into your lap. Take this idea a little farther now... your intent has just altered reality in some way by changing or nudging a possible outcome. If you hadn't done the spell, would you still have gotten three job offers? No one can know the answer for sure, but we do know that your reality cannot remain unaffected when you focus your intent.

We also know that the more specific a spell, the more specific the result. Can this be coincidence? I don't believe in coincidences personally, but I do know that unintended results can sometimes come from spells that are too vague. I'm sure you've found this to be the case as well—"I want a boyfriend," you say, and burn some "love" incense. Sure, you may get your boyfriend, but he may turn out to be a jerk or worse. You may get so many offers for dates that you begin to wonder if you're wearing a transparent shirt. Is this the kind of reality you want to create for yourself?

Yes, you are creating your own reality when you work magic. Even in the mundane world, when you paint the bathroom or choose clothing for the office or plant some flowers, you have created a new reality for yourself. The bathroom is now freshly painted and different than it was before, your coworkers or employer will have different reactions to your choice of clothing, and your yard will look different, too (assuming the plants don't die immediately—but that's a different kind of different).

Let's explore this a little more on a magical level. If reality bites, you can do many things mundanely to try to change this, such as getting a new job, dumping the crummy boyfriend, and so on. But what "cosmic forces" bring these things into your life if you haven't done anything to attract them? Why has your car been broken into four times but your neighbors' cars untouched? Conversely, why does your life seem "lucky" while the coworker in the cubicle next to yours is constantly having unforeseen problems? Sure, it could be paying for a past life experience or something, but this could also be how you are affecting your reality right now, whether you know it or not.

Do you focus on the pleasant things in life, or do you let every small problem bring you down? Do you view your life as chaotic or generally peaceful? I once knew a woman who had the most chaotic life I've ever encountered. In one day she had car problems, had to take time off work because her daughter was caught with drugs in school, and less-than-skilled painters had come to her condo and somehow painted the doors and windows shut so she couldn't get into her house. Looking at how she handles everything in her life, frenetically and with an "it figures this would happen to me" mentality, I think she may have been creating an area of chaos around herself so that these things were actually more likely to happen.

So now we come back to quantum theory that we explored in the first chapter. "Oh, man, not this again!" you plead. But check it out—quantum theory helps explain why weird stuff like an "unlucky" person follows scientific laws.

John Gribbon, in his book *In Search of Schrödinger's Cat*, has a terrific example of how these things might happen:

> Think of a stone dropped on the ground. When it hits the ground, the energy of its motion is converted into heat. But if we put an identical stone on the ground and warm it by the same amount, it doesn't jump up into the air. Why not? In the case of the falling stone, an orderly form of motion (all the atoms and molecules falling in the same direction) is turned into a disordered form of motion. If you put disordered heat energy into a stone it cannot use that energy to create an orderly movement of all the molecules in the stone so that they jump together upward.
>
> Or can it? [Thermodynamics scientist Ludwig] Boltzmann... said that such a remarkable occurrence *could* happen, but it is extremely unlikely. In the same way, as a result of random movement of air molecules it *could* happen that all of the air in the room might suddenly concentrate in the

corners...but such a possibility is so unlikely that for all practical purposes it can be ignored.

While it's extremely unlikely that all the air in the room will suddenly migrate to the corners (at least, let's hope it is!), this idea says something important about probability ruling the universe. Reality is not so concrete as some scientists would like, and the moment-by-moment actions of everything around us are constantly being determined by chance. Or luck if you prefer. And we know how easy it can be to nudge things through a magic working, or even strong thoughts.

So let's take this farther. What is the chance that you'll get up in the morning and your car will have become an elephant, you will suddenly have grown a lovely pair of wings, and all plants are now bright purple instead of green? So incredibly tiny that it's probably not measurable. But it *could* happen. It's not *impossible*. Nothing is impossible. Reality is fluid and ever-changing, right down to the subatomic level.

If reality is fluid and ever-changing, then what forces influence these changes? The random bouncing of atoms and subatomic particles off of each other? The will of God? Observations made by all forms of life? The energy and intent of human beings? Perhaps none of these things form our consensual reality. Perhaps all of them do. Since this book was written for human beings, let's focus for now on how humans can work to alter reality.

I enjoy the book *Medicine for the Earth* by Sandra Ingerman very much. In it, you are learning to create not only your own reality, but even your own creation story as you sense the universe to have started. Reading this book has been like a sheer white curtain of peace and sense drifting over me in a light breeze. I can immediately feel the divine energies wash in as I read each chapter, and the exercises are terrific. She uses her history of shamanistic techniques as a student of Michael Harner and takes you closer to the experience of becoming the divine yourself, able to change the world.

Ingerman's methods of becoming hollow and opening yourself up to the divine light enable you to physically transform poisoned water into safe water, which naturally translates to a diseased body or anything else that needs to be healed. Not allowing yourself to be chained to consensual reality enables you to perform what most would consider miracles, and science proves this again and again—as we have seen in the previous chapter.

All this talk about consensual reality, however, can make some people uncomfortable. If we are basically thumbing our noses at what most of the world understands to be real, does that slip into mental illness? If we have visions, or hear the voices of spirits and deities, or believe we can change the world with magic alone, can the men in the little white coats be far behind?

It appears that our "modern Western society" has somehow determined that people who see and hear these things, who believe these things, who experience a different "reality" on a regular basis must be insane. We don't understand people like this, so they must be locked up as a danger to themselves and others, the psychiatric experts claim. Consider what happened to Wiccan community leader Oz when she sought counseling during an impending divorce. The psychiatrist said to her, "Your husband tells me you think you're a Witch. Do you? You know, we have some people in the hospital here who suffer from that delusion. It's a very serious problem."

To say that he has an utter and total lack of understanding about what Witches are is quite an understatement. But it reveals something else—a large portion of the psychiatric professional community has decided that someone who thinks he can do magic and affect reality must be delusional. In the burning times and the American witch hunts it was considered "hysteria" (the word originating from the Greek *hystera*, meaning "womb," indicating that it was thought to be a woman's disease stemming from the uterus). It should also be noted that ours is the only society to make such a judgment, since most other cultures look upon those who experience visions, hear voices, and experience altered states of consciousness on a regular basis as holy people. They are the shamans, the medicine people, the priests and priestesses, not the insane.

It's interesting that while some Christian and other mainstream holy people have reportedly experienced things like visions and auditory hallucinations, these are somehow regarded as part of their ecstatic religious experience, while those practicing shamanic and indigenous religions are often seen as charlatans, delusional, or schizophrenic (or any combination the shrink decides upon). Thus we see a "professional" labeling of what is not experienced, or even understood fully by the psychiatrist. What is not understood is considered false or even dangerous, both negative conclusions about something that most magic workers find to be a positive influence on their lives.

Of course, not everyone who hallucinates maintains his grip on daily reality, and not everyone who hears voices is listening to God. There are certainly many disturbed individuals who cannot function in society because of visual or auditory hallucinations, and true schizophrenia is often manifest in bizarre and paranoid imaginings that cannot be corroborated by anyone. But such experiences are very different from those of the shaman who goes on a deep spirit journey Sunday evening and then goes off to work as a lawyer or office manager or short-order cook the next morning.

It may be some kind of difference of degrees, especially within the magic worker who has self-doubt (don't we all have a little bit?), but I think that as long as you can interact with others in your society in a reasonable way, a little reality bending never hurt anybody and can be beneficial at times. When you think about it, the entire movie industry is built on playing with reality, but nobody ever tried to institutionalize Steven Spielberg or the staff of Industrial Light and Magic (you've gotta love that name).

While some famous artists like Vincent van Gogh, Charles Mingus, and William Blake were institutionalized, practiced self-mutilation, or suffered from depression so severe they committed suicide, they also contributed masterpieces of words or music or paint and canvas to our world that are admired by everyone, adding artistry to our consensual reality by going outside of it to create wonders. An interesting paradox.

This is akin to what the magic worker encounters. By not listening to "logic" and "reason," she is able to travel in shamanistic journeys to the underworld, to heal with the power of the mind alone, to cast spells that change reality, to speak with dead ancestors, receive visions from deities and spirits, and many other "fantastical" things that scientists and psychiatrists explain away or put in the "delusion" box. It is when we doubt our ability to do this that the magic is lost.

When I first began studying Witchcraft in the late 1970s, I read an old grimoire that said, "If any doubt whatsoever enters your mind while working the spell, its effects will be ruined." Naturally this made me overly paranoid in the other direction, but the point is the same—you must have faith that you can alter reality or you probably will not be able to. Faith is the cornerstone of all religion, to believe in what cannot be scientifically demonstrated. Magic is also bolstered by faith, for without your force of will and belief that what you're doing is real, even the most carefully crafted spell will flop like a deflated balloon from the lack of power and intent behind it.

Also remember that your version of what is real and everyone else's version of what is real are probably extremely diverse. This is certainly not to imply that you're wrong or delusional, or worse. As we saw in the example earlier of the traffic accident, ask any number of people something and you'll get the same number of answers, all different, but all with varying degrees of validity according to the consensual reality. The point is that if you have seen some of your spells come to fruition, have gone on some spirit journeys, or have received guidance from spirits and deities, you understand these things to be just as real as a bowl of ice cream, even if your next-door neighbor thinks you're nuts.

But now it's time to stretch your magical muscles. It's time to go beyond what you read in books, to go beyond the safe place that others have explored before you. Get off the neatly paved highway, turn away even from the rutted dirt road—you need to find that bit of wilderness that few people have seen, or that perhaps you are the first to discover. Shake things up, take an evening or a week or a year or a lifetime to say, "What if? . . ."

Look at the room around you or, if you're lucky enough to be reading this outside, look at your nearby landscape. See that chair or tree or bird or cat or patch of grass? Is it really there, or is consensual reality at work? What if you could lift that veneer and see the chasm, the chaos that is below the consensual reality? I think this is why virtually all of us don't do this—it would be too confusing or frightening to exist within for long. The consensual reality is understandable, safe, familiar, our home. But from this infinite chaos came our world, or so pretty much every religion on Earth tells us. Neith came from Nun, God spoke the word, Frog-Man brought mud up from the waters to make the land, Lakshmi and Aphrodite came from the churning milky foam of the oceans . . . and it was all good. It made sense from what could not be fathomed. Whether humans made up the stories or these things really happened, it doesn't matter—order was still created from disorder and created the consensual reality we understand today.

As an experienced priest, priestess, shaman, Witch, et cetera, you've reached the limit of the conventional. It's time to stick your toe into the churning foam, peek for a moment into the bottom-less chasm, pull back the curtain a tiny bit to reveal the Wizard of Oz. But this magic is not a humbug, it is the unknowable, the chaos that begets all and can drive people to madness because they are too limited to perceive it all. But if we take it slowly, bit by bit, we can gently begin to explore this strange new world and work with it with minimal danger.

Reality is an illusion.

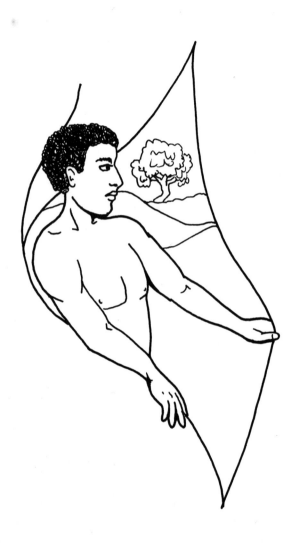

3

The Veil Between the Worlds

"Those who dream by day are cognizant of many things which escape those who dream only by night." —EDGAR ALLAN POE

"Why is the Veil there? I don't know. Why is the Sun above? It just is. Not trying to sound like a smartass. That's my honest answer." —M. MACHA NIGHTMARE

PERCEPTIONS OF THE VEIL VARY WIDELY, AND ONE COULD ALmost suppose that the Veil appears different to every individual. Opinions that I've heard in the Pagan and magical communities run the gambit from "what Veil?" to views that it's a complex barrier wall constructed to keep "fleshies" on one side and the spirit world on the other. The slippery thing about trying to describe the Veil is that, as mentioned above, it appears different to everyone and there's no way to know if people are seeing the same Veil or many different ones.

Some magic workers that I asked described the Veil as made up of multiple layers, one on top of another. One woman said that when she saw an unhealthy spot in the Veil, it was like "rotting cardboard," with various layers of gunk flaking off and crumbling. Others have seen a luminous translucent membrane, a shimmering gauzy fabric, a grayish smoky cloud, or a strong feeling of an astral wall with no visual imagery attached.

The Veil is depicted at Reclaiming's annual Spiral Dance in San Francisco as sheer curtains that you pass through when going between the lobby of the building and the ritual space. Artists Laura Kemp and Sara Boore created layers and layers of translucent white fabric, hanging mazelike from the ceiling, decorated in some places with skulls and skeletons to add to the Samhain effect and remind us that we are passing into the realms of the dead. There are breaks in the fabric through which participants pass, but they are staggered so that you are forced to wander back and forth as you find your path through the Veil. It also serves to remind everyone that we are going into sacred space (or out, if you're heading for the mundane realm of the bathroom), and that this journey from one side to the other is not an easy one. This simple prop is every bit as important as any candles, incense, or music to the nature of this ritual, and it's interesting to see the Veil portrayed this way.

Another opinion, that of M. Macha NightMare, Elder and priestess in the Reclaiming Tradition, is: "I guess I'd describe it more as a 'differentness,' the feeling of the Other Side, not so much as a membrane or veil. Just a differentness of feeling." Arhuaine, a longtime member of the online magic community, says: "I think that the 'veil' is nothing more than a psychological barrier; it's that lit-

tle voice of logic that says 'this isn't real,' and so therefore prevents you from accessing these other realms."

In many shamanic traditions, crossing to the spirit world involves going through a tunnel, a cloud, a door formed from a symbol, or simply exiting the corporeal body and being in another realm immediately. If we take the Veil to be the ineffable something that separates everyday reality from the spirit world(s), then the definitions and descriptions are infinite. It then assumes a pigeonhole of divine proportions—"it is everything and nothing, different for everyone who perceives it."

As we saw in chapter 2, reality is in the eye of the beholder, so it seems to me that all of these opinions are equally valid. We are taking something mysterious and transcendent and filtering it through the perceptions of individuals, each with his or her own histories, experiences, biases, expectations, and ways of seeing the universe. When you take all that into account, it actually makes more sense that the Veil would seem different to each person. This is not to say that separate people going to view the Veil cannot see and experience the same thing. It only suggests that the Veil is something beyond the casual understanding and perception of most people.

It also suggests that there may be many Veils, each one to a different realm, or that the Veil varies by physical location, or that it appears differently according to the viewer's own energies and skills. I personally have seen many variations of the Veil, each one pretty much conforming to what someone else has described.

I go in with expectations and they are met, so perhaps the Veil is something like Heaven, a thing that appears to the person as what they're expecting—Christians see Jesus and the Pearly Gates, Witches see Avalon and the God and Goddess waiting for them, and so on. Near-death experiences have proven this idea as well. A researcher recently interviewed hundreds of children from around the world who had been revived from the brink of death. All of them saw what their culture said they'd see, with Christian chil-

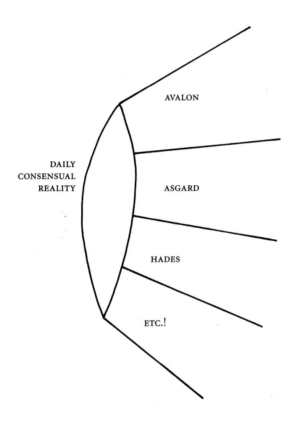

The Veil is a portal to many astral realms and may appear different to everyone.

dren seeing Jesus, African children seeing their ancestors and local deities, Buddhist children seeing Buddha...you see the pattern here.

Speaking of death, one of the most common ways a Witch or Wiccan crosses the Veil (or at least works with the Veil) is during Samhain rituals. At the Spiral Dance, and probably at many other Samhain rituals around the world, participants are mentally guided through the Veil so that they can communicate with deceased loved ones, contact the spirit of a potential future son or daughter, or receive messages from the divine.

In my experience, the typical Samhain trip is a gentle one involving only mild trance and meditation, not the potentially dangerous working of actually having your own spirit cross over into the spirit realms. This type of undertaking (no pun intended) is dealt with in more depth in the next chapter on shamanism and should not be attempted alone. You may not be able to find your way back, and even experienced priests and priestesses can become lost and/or have trouble restoring balance when deep workings are attempted. M. Macha NightMare described to me one such incident and the results of crossing over to the other side as a death priestess helping a friend to pass across:

> I'm not sure if you could say I actually *crossed*. I went a very long way from this world to another plane, but I didn't think it was time for me to cross over and completely leave this world. It kind of felt like the circle and the chanting in the room where my body was figuratively held me by the ankles to keep me from getting lost and not returning. After I came

back to the room, it still took a lot of time, and heavy food, for me to really come back. I craved beef and a chocolate shake; I didn't get it then but I did get some food.

I also had intense energy work massage, then later gentler, more healing massage. The second was done by a person I'm magically close to, and she got lots of images from my experience that I hadn't previously described to her. She got them from touch and energy sensing.

Within the month, I was privileged to be in attendance at a birthing, and that went a long way toward bringing me back, or restoring the balance in my life.

Obviously, crossing the Veil is hard and demanding work, which is true of any Veilwork, and also true of many of the techniques in this book. Sometimes even the most experienced priests and priestesses have trouble finding the road, let alone finding a road map that will guide them safely along it. These things have no maps—other than the ones we create as we go. Others can describe what they experience, which may or may not match what we experience, so it's hard to tell if someone else's opinions are illuminating or limiting.

But where are we traveling to? When we "cross the Veil," where do we go? One answer is to the spirit realm of the deceased, where we go when we die. Another answer, not exclusive of the first one, is that we pass into the underworld of the shaman where we meet our power animals, receive guidance, and fight demons. Another realm that might be found on the other side is the land of Faerie. Some would say that alternate or parallel realities are what you find on the other side, or even portals to other worlds or planets, like a wormhole in space. Maybe it's the world of the Old Gods and you're visiting Olympus or Asgard, where anything can happen. All of these answers are just as real and valid as the next; it all depends on what the traveler is looking for.

One easy answer seems to be that we cross over to the amorphous astral plane, where all possibilities are at once real and imminent, existing together in harmony. We are simply seeing one piece of that plane at a time, depending on which door you use and who is walking through it. What do you think? Have you only experienced one portal through the Veil or found many ways to cross? Do you always find the same landscape, or is it different every time? It can be really helpful to keep a journal of your travels, creating a sort of personal road map as you go. Then you can look back and compare old experiences while exploring new possibilities of what it means to cross the Veil.

Aside from simply imagining that you cross this threshold when you do a meditation or mental journey, there are many ways to cross the Veil (no, I'm not even remotely suggesting suicide). Outside of the states of altered consciousness that help the shaman or Witch across, the magic worker can work consciously in a ritual framework to open a portal or hole in the Veil through which to work or to allow things through *(carefully!)* to this side of it.

There has been some talk of certain groups forcibly ripping holes in the Veil to allow more magic to come through into this world and to allow them to do magic workings more easily. Obviously, this is incredibly foolhardy! Shredding the Veil, whether physical, metaphoric, or something else, would result in any number of harmful things, including allowing malevolent entities to come through (either on purpose or accidentally), increasing the incidence of hauntings and poltergeist activities, loss of loved ones in comas and otherwise close to passing over, natural or other disasters, and even if nothing else, it would cause mass confusion and chaos in the mundane world.

All of this is not to say that it is never a good idea to open a portal in the Veil. I am only talking about the dangers of ripping holes in it carelessly and assuming you have any kind of authority to justify such a ragged and dangerous act. I will probably be criticized for being alarmist throughout the course of this book, but I know that there will be some people out there who lack the judgment and/or experience to handle some of the things found in these pages, and I hope to dissuade anyone from attempting some of these workings without at least the proper training and support from other knowledgeable people.

Assuming you do have those years of experience under your belt and the support of several others who wish to attempt opening a portal (not tearing a hole) through the Veil, such a working is possible and a useful skill to have, especially if you do a lot of traveling through it or have contacts on the other side with which you would like to communicate more clearly.

I asked several people how they do Veilwork, and how a person might be able to open such a portal. Rialian, someone I know to have considerable talents in this area, suggested that people should start out by finding ley lines, points where ley lines intersect, natural power spots, Faerie rings, and so on to help make the working easier than if you just pick the middle of your living room. He says:

> Personally, I would try walking the land first...find the areas that pull the way you need them to. This way you may come across areas that would have been known for faery "trods" and activities. Then see what you get...working with the area gives the best result... Everyone seems to think that there is a set way or ways...there is not. I think it depends on the way you interact with the space, and the flows of the land.
>
> I have found the walking around a "well" to be a start there...walking around, feeling oneself going into the Earth.... and see what comes from it. When you are "deep" enough, follow the flows to where you need to go...see what feels right to do this with. There is magick in the walking of the trods.
>
> Some of the best areas to do this is the areas of "crossover" in forests...if you know of an area with really good underground fungal growth, that is the best place to do this... there is some truth to the statement that the mushroom rings are an opening to faery.

Those who perceive a real barrier rather than a metaphor when they encounter the Veil may also perceive that it can use a little help sometimes. Efforts to forcibly open the Veil may cause lasting damage to its structure, as can amateur efforts to manipulate it, psychic battles, world disasters and wars, pollution and desecration of sacred places, and probably many other things I've left out here.

Assuming that you leave gifts when you gather sacred plants, and thank the deities that have helped you along the way, it makes sense to honor and heal the Veil as an entity or sacred thing as well. By healing and cleansing the Veil, you align yourself more with its energies and can work with it more easily and safely. Even if it's only a metaphor to you, recognizing and honoring its purpose in the world may help you understand and work with it that much more easily. Cleansing the Veil also helps others to cross this membrane—it's easier to see through a clean window and walk through a hallway free of spiderwebs and debris.

Here is a Veil-cleansing ritual given to me in 1999 by an Internet friend whom I've since lost touch with. In her notes to me, she says, "This is pretty much a compilation of the rituals my friends and I have done, using elements from different rituals that worked well. With Veilwork you always have to be very flexible—it never behaves like you plan it to."

A few years back I did this ritual in my open women's coven, and a modified version of this ritual as part of a large Mabon celebration, which, instead of the usual harvest and feasting focus, centered on the transfer of power from the Harvest Mother to the Dark Mother and worked on preparing ourselves and the Veil for Samhain. This ritual is better for smaller, more tightly knit groups, to avoid problems such as accidental harm to the Veil, chaotic energy entering the circle, people not being grounded well enough and being adversely affected, and so on.

*During the Veil-cleansing ritual, have everyone follow what the
Veil has told them it needs, which may include holding it, sending
energy, stroking it, brushing off astral "gunk," singing to it, and
so on.*

Depending on how many people are participating, you will
need one or more yards of gauze, preferably silk, to represent the
Veil. You will also need appropriate incense, olive oil in a small
dish, a minimum of one stone for each quarter (the more stones
the better to help ground the energy), a symbolic World Tree (a
bonsai tree, a houseplant, or even a charged staff are all good for
this, and it should be placed in the center of the circle), sage or
other smudging incense for the participants, and pure springwater
or any other clean and natural water.

The best time for this ritual is on the new or full moon, preferably at night to minimize distractions. Begin by speaking to the spirits of the land where you are, offering libations and praise as you describe what you're about to do and making sure they're okay with it. Open yourself up to the resident spirits who appear friendly and helpful, and ask for their assistance in healing the Veil. Welcome them with whatever gift feels appropriate, such as milk or other food, music, drumming, incense, and so on.

Smudge everyone in your group before casting the circle as you normally would. Make sure it's a tight casting to help ground everyone as well as possible before starting any Veilwork. Now call in the quarters, using the entire group or using individuals as quarter anchors if they feel up to the job. If using individuals, at least have the rest of the group whisper the element name as it is invoked so that everyone is "there" with the elements. Go around the circle and quarters more than once if necessary—use your best judgment.

Now lead everyone in some kind of grounding and centering exercise, whatever works best for you and your group. Deep breathing and a visualization of the World Tree inside each person works very well. Emphasize the idea that you will be handling the Veil and bridging the worlds, using the World Tree as a focus.

At this point, have everyone stand up as they maintain their focus on the World Tree and make sure they stay in this meditative state. One by one in turn, wrap each member of the circle in the Veil fabric, covering their head if possible. Hold it there for a moment, then have them turn counterclockwise as you unwrap them to "spin off" any mental clutter and the mundane world. Then anoint their third eye with the olive oil and say, "You have other ways of seeing." This will symbolize the internal Veil within them.

When everyone in the circle has been wrapped and anointed, call out to the Great Spirit, God and Goddess—whomever you usually call out to during ritual—and ask it/him/her to help and guide you. Now take the fabric and have everyone hold it, addressing the Veil as you might a sick friend. Stroke it, touch it, speak to it, and see where it needs to be healed and cleansed. Each person may divine this in a different way, or you could be surprised and have a group consensus. Have a minute or two of silence so that everyone can open themselves up to the Veil and get impressions of what it needs. When everyone seems ready, have them describe what they felt, saw, or heard. Follow the instructions as best you can for a few minutes, then take the fabric Veil and wash it with the pure water, washing away any remaining sickness or general nasty bits.

To finish the ritual, lay out or fold the Veil fabric carefully and make sure everyone is feeling okay and grounded, doing additional grounding or meditations as needed to avoid "floaters" in your group. When you're all ready and together, thank all the powers and spirits you invoked and asked assistance of, open the circle as you normally would, and leave an offering to the land. The fabric should be carefully set aside for any future magic workings, especially Veilwork, but do not use it as an altar cloth where it might get wax or dirt on it.

Now that we have cleansed and honored the Veil, we can begin working with it more in earnest and forming portals to the other side if need be. As the examples of the dirty window or hallway above illustrate, cleansing the Veil is the first step to being able to go through it. The healthy membrane free of debris and injury is able to stretch, to breathe, to be shaped, and to be passed through. Even if you view the Veil as mere metaphor, washing away the gunk associated with it removes part of that mental barrier, making it easier to cross beyond.

If you have land that you wish to use for this purpose, you can create a "hot spot" or anchor point of semipermanence through which you can do your workings. In ancient times, caves, springs, wells, hilltops, and other sacred sites were natural points where the Veil was thinner. If you have the opportunity to visit a place like this, take some time (by yourself or with your magic partners if possible) to feel the energy of the place and become familiar with it. Especially notice what you feel regarding the Veil—you may also choose to visit these places on auspicious days to amplify the effect. Don't try to do any workings at these places the first time you visit; just get a feeling for the general energy of the location, note any differences between the spot and the mundane world, and remember to walk around and note any particular power spots or thin spots in the Veil. Write down everything you find, get opinions from your group if others are with you, and get as familiar with the feeling of Veil thinning as you can for future reference.

When you are ready to create your own anchor point, find the best spot that's naturally attuned to this kind of work and be sure you ask permission of the local land spirits before starting. It's also a very good idea to own the land so that you can control who passes by the place—that way you don't have curious people wandering about there, perhaps attracted to the spot without knowing why. As with any important working, cleanse and purify both the place and yourself before starting, and set up the location in advance with everything you'll need.

Begin your ritual as you usually would, perhaps calling the Watchtowers or however your "ritual template" dictates you begin, but make sure you cast the circle (or otherwise create your sacred space) especially tightly, anchoring it well to the physical Earth plane. I like to do a triple circle casting when doing ethereal work like this, ending it by firmly planting the tip of my athame into the ground. Begin the working by addressing the Veil as a sentient en-

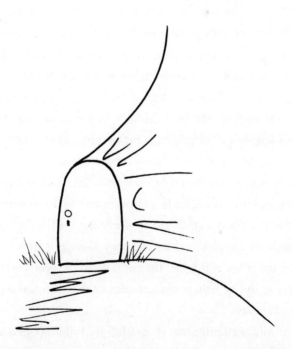

An established portal in the Veil can look like a conventional door in an anchor point or can be much more organic in its appearance.

tity, explaining why you will be creating the anchor point and being as friendly and understanding as possible, as if you're speaking to a very highly respected Elder.

When you can clearly sense the fabric of the Veil and receive a positive response to your working, reach out and touch it, stroking the Veil and learning all you can about its makeup (no, not cosmetics) in that location. Using an energy sigil or other technique, gently stretch a bit of the Veil out and attach it to the Earth, which will look sort of like pulling on a nylon stocking to make a convex cone shape. You may perceive this differently. This anchor can then be fitted with a sort of astral door that can be opened as needed by you or your group, which is much easier to work with than creating a whole new door every time you do Veilwork.

When you and the Veil are both ready, it's time for your first attempt at opening a door or portal at your anchor point. See if you can determine what is on the other side before doing this. In other words, look through the peephole before unlocking your deadbolt and opening the door. If it's obvious that malevolent or overeager entities are waiting on the other side, close the ritual and try again another time when it's safer. If it appears safe to do so, very gently and cautiously open a small rift in the fabric and allow a little of that energy exchange to occur. You may also get a better look at what's on the other side while the rift is open. Be prepared to let it snap shut again, or help it close if necessary if you sense trouble coming your way.

If your initial attempt was successful, try holding open a larger door for a longer period of time, making sure you are able to close it up again quickly in case of an emergency. Continue this work over the course of several weeks or months to become familiar with this portion of the Veil and how the portal will work. When you are satisfied that your location will not be especially prone to malevolent attacks or forced entry, it's time to create your semi-permanent door. I say *semipermanent* because *permanent* is a really long time, and neither you nor anyone else can safely determine that this door will remain in good hands for eternity. Misuse of it, from either side of the Veil, could lead to disaster and a lot of repair and cleanup work from future generations, assuming that they will know how to fix the problem.

At any rate, to create your semipermanent door or portal, you can either simply manifest the image of a contemporary door in the opening you create, complete with lock and key, or you can create a more organic form of seal that you can open with certain commands, energy matrix keys, or other methods of your choosing. Feel free to get creative with your door and method of unlocking it; just make sure you work into the arrangement that if left unused for a certain amount of time (days, weeks, years) the door will naturally dissolve back into the Veil. When you need to do frequent Veilwork, just unlock the door with your keys and you will have easier access to the realms on the other side.

If working with a group, you can see who is best able to hold and control this door, using perhaps one person to the left and one to the right of the opening, and get right up to the threshold of it to peer inside or contact an entity. If serious work is required, such as locating a lost soul or the need to find a specific entity, you or one of your group may decide to cross over astrally through the door. Have two people working the portal or door, one person

Working with other knowledgeable people facilitates difficult and/or complex rituals, such as Veilcrossing, so that the primary priest/ess is freed to concentrate on the task at hand.

doing the traveling, and everyone else working hard to keep the traveler grounded on this side to avoid unfortunate circumstances such as spirit possession, becoming seriously lost on the other side, disorientation, or even coma or death. Obviously, this is nothing to play with and should only be attempted by experienced magic workers with the help of others of similar caliber.

Now that you have become somewhat familiar with Veilwork, you may start to recognize weak spots in the Veil more easily, or sense certain times when the Veil is thinner more often, or detect portals that other people have set up as you travel. Your experience and newly heightened awareness may also alert you to situations where entities or inexperienced people have caused a rift in the Veil that you will be able to help repair.

No matter how you see the Veil, being able to work with it and work with realms on the other side is one of the basic techniques of Witchcraft, shamanism, and other forms of ecstatic worship. As we will see in the next chapter, there are many ways to cross over and do this spirit work through altered states of consciousness, made easier now that we've laid the basic groundwork for handling the Veil and creating portals through it. Just remember to use your head, get reality checks from others, and treat the Veil with the respect it deserves.

4

Shamanism and Ecstatic Worship

"Aboriginal medicine men, so far from being rogues, charlatans or ignoramuses, are men of high *degree; that is, men who have taken a degree in the secret life beyond that taken by most adult males— a step which implies discipline, mental training, courage and perseverance."*   —A. P. ELKIN

"Your biggest obstacles in this will be cultural and social, not shamanic, for we live in the very civilization that persecuted and destroyed those who possessed the ancient knowledge."

—MICHAEL HARNER

"If we look beyond the numerous and confusing present-day notions about shamans and witches… intriguing commonalities emerge."

—FELICITAS D. GOODMAN

THE WORD *SHAMAN* CONJURES UP ALL KINDS OF IMMEDIATE mental imagery. I would hazard a guess that most Western minds, especially those in America, think of people decked out in feathers and beads, using a drum or rattle and singing chants in some unfamiliar tongue. The word *shaman,* however, comes to us from Siberia, and the varied shamanic techniques of achieving altered states of consciousness to do magic workings and spirit healings are pretty much universal ancient practices not limited to any continent, language, skin color, or religion.

Mircea Eliade, in his groundbreaking and seminal book *Shamanism: Archaic Techniques of Ecstasy,* offers many technical definitions of shamanism. The simplest and perhaps best, based on the wide variations to be found around the world, is that it's a "technique of ecstasy." I would add to this that it is a system of spirituality based on working with otherworldly beings (gods, power animals, loas, and so forth) through some kind of altered state of consciousness and is primarily used for healing others. At times, but not always, some kind of physical ordeal is part of the ceremony, primarily to help attain the detachment from the body and altered state of consciousness necessary for shamanic journeying to the spirit realms.

How is the shaman different from the Witch? It appears that the shaman is more "outside" and the Witch is more "inside." The shaman achieves an altered state of consciousness and travels to the divine to work with them. Modern Witches, ignoring for the moment medieval accounts of flying ointments and traveling to astral Sabbats, generally work within a circle and call the deity in to them. Raising power can be considered a mild state of altered consciousness, but the shaman is truly "out there," and his body is for the most part unrelated to the work his mind is doing. But this is a comparison of the more ceremonial "traditional" Wiccan and the shaman. Many "eclectic" Witches and other magic workers incorporate many shamanic techniques in their work. These techniques may include (but are certainly not limited to) drumming and music, ecstatic dance, psychoactive drugs and herbs, the sweat lodge, and deep guided meditation.

An important distinction of shamanism from a particular religion that Eliade finds in his research is that shamanism generally coexists with other forms of spirituality in a culture and does not replace it. In *Shamanism*, we see that the shaman is the community healer and spirit worker, but is not necessarily the priest who leads the main religious rituals. For example, in the American Appalachian mountains, you might find an elderly "wise woman" dispensing folk remedies from her home, but she still goes to church faithfully every Sunday morning. She is the healer, not the priest.

Thus, shamanism can be a part of any system of magic—it is not limited to boxes and labels. The ecstatic technique of worship is found all over the world and in every religion, even though some would blanch, or even be offended, if you tried to call them "shamans." Certainly some systems of belief are far more shamanic than others, such as many Native American traditions, but "shamanism" is not connected to any one culture or way of worshiping the divine.

If someone comes to you and says she is a shaman, or her path is shamanism, ask her what her larger religious framework is or ask for a definition of what she means by shamanism. Being a shaman doesn't simply mean going out into the wilderness and shaking a rattle or beating a drum—it needs a cultural or spiritual context. Who is she calling to? Who is she doing the working for? Where did she learn her techniques? Was she called by the gods and shown the path, or did she simply think it would be "cool" to be a shaman?

Another important finding in Eliade's book is that most often the shaman is what modern Witches would consider "self-initiated" and does not go through a separate ritual to "become" a shaman. He or she simply *is* a shaman by a spiritual calling and by initiation from the gods—any work with elder shamans is the more practical training of learning how to work with the divine, local medicinal plants and their uses, how to journey outside the body safely, and so on.

Traditionally, the shaman is only called by the gods, often violently with near-death experiences such as being hit by lightning or a vision so intense it paralyzes him for several days. The "little death" that most cultures deem necessary for the true shaman to emerge points to the idea of "the wounded healer," a person who must truly understand injury, disease, and death to be able to deal with them successfully. Generally, the person who simply wishes to become a shaman without being called or being given power by the gods is not considered a real shaman by the community and is rejected as soon as a more powerful, "real" shaman is available.

This is also true of those paths and techniques that, while they don't call themselves "shamanic," are certainly manifest in ecstatic worship involving altered states of consciousness. Take for example the case of the snake handler sects of Christianity, primarily found in the American southern Pentecostal or charismatic movements. Following a passage in the Bible that (paraphrased) states they will be unharmed by serpent and poisons if they truly believe in the power of Jesus, they sing and dance frenetically until they are in a trance, handling poisonous snakes and allowing themselves to be bitten, sometimes drinking poisonous substances like kerosene, and speaking in tongues (also called glossolalia). Certainly a preacher who was unable to do these things would fall out of favor over time and be replaced by one who could, especially since it is his inspiration that gets the rest of the congregants whipped up into the ecstatic frenzy that enables them to participate as well.

Glossolalia, the interesting aforementioned phenomenon, occurs when the congregation is inspired and whipped up by the priest or preacher. They feel filled with the Holy Spirit or possessed by it, and begin to issue forth what appear to be nonsense syllables and words, often repeated single sounds in a stream; the speaker often stands with hands upraised and eyes closed, appearing to be in a trance or trancelike state.

Dr. Felicitas D. Goodman, author of the excellent book on shamanism *Where the Spirits Ride the Wind,* originally came to shamanism through her work as a linguist and translator working on the phenomenon of glossolalia. Through phonetic analysis of glossolalia examples from all over the world, she found that, while not a true language, the examples did feature strikingly similar uses of sounds and repetition patterns, no matter what the culture practicing it. This is an interesting finding, suggesting that these people may actually be contacting the collective consciousness during glossolalia sessions, if not the Supreme Being itself.

So through altered states of consciousness, ecstatic worship techniques, physical manifestations of "the Holy Spirit" such as glossolalia, and other examples of spiritual mind over matter, we see that the practitioner (either a trained shaman or one using shamanic practices) is unafraid to explore other realities and incorporate them into his or her way of worshiping the divine. This is the common thread among such seemingly disparate groups as charismatic Christians, modern Wiccans, and traditional tribal shamans. Even such "conservative" groups as the Shakers and Quakers receive ecstatic physical signs of the Holy Spirit—the involuntary tremors of the body during worship that gave these groups their names.

There are many other techniques of ecstatic worship and routes through which the magic worker can explore rituals involving altered states of consciousness. Masks are an incredibly ancient way for humans to become something they're not, either mentally for themselves, outwardly for the benefit of others, or both. Many ancient cultures used masks, some with hinged jaws or other parts, to depict and to become certain deities during a ritual.

In the Stone Age paintings of Lascaux and Les Trois Frères, we see men wearing bird and stag masks as they work their magic rituals fifteen thousand years ago or more. Masks have been found dating back to prehistoric Britain and ancient Egypt in the shapes of animals or animal-headed gods. Virtually every culture in the world has used masks as part of their religious practices, and many still do today.

The mask can represent an animal, an archetype of nature, a deity archetype, the persona of a deity, or an abstract concept. The mask is the connection to these things, something that can be donned to help the shaman, priest/ess, or celebrant become something he or she ordinarily isn't. Of course, there are various levels of depth to putting on a mask. The child at Halloween dons a mask to be someone else for one evening, but it is primarily theatrical. The hunter may wear an animal mask to fool the prey or to become one with its spirit (or both). Shamans, priests, or priestesses may put on a mask to invoke that deity inside themselves and speak through the mouth of the mask to others as that deity. Those who are unable to fully take in a deity during a ritual because of self-consciousness or other barriers may be able to truly become and host that spirit while wearing a mask. Behind the mask we are someone else to another person, whatever our intent while wearing it.

Mask work has been one of the major ways in which my Egyptian temple has worked with the Netjeru, or Egyptian pantheon of gods and goddesses. It is through the mask of Bast that I have been able to work with Her most closely and truly experience what Her energy is like (more about this kind of work in a subsequent chapter). All our masks have been made with love, care, and with the artists allowing that spirit to come through them into the mask. I imagine that is how anyone making a sacred mask, especially one depicting a particular deity, would create one.

Carefully made masks are important to other traditions as well, and the book *Sacred Mask, Sacred Dance* by Evan John Jones describes the Craft tradition the author belongs to, which centers on these masks. Each member of the group dons a different animal mask, which enables taking on the persona and spirit of that animal and bringing its teachings into the circle. Many other groups may also don masks, either as part of the formal ritual or as a whimsical accessory to it. At one Imbolc ritual I participated in, the lead characters donned masks to help the audience understand who was who more easily and to add to the theatrical drama of the performance—we could just as easily have done the ritual without

The Deer Dance is traditional to some Native American tribes and mimics the movements of the deer as it honors its spirit.

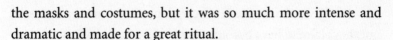

the masks and costumes, but it was so much more intense and dramatic and made for a great ritual.

We see that masks can be an important part of ritual, especially when we are attempting to become someone or something outside of our mundane selves. When the shaman wishes to become one with the spirit of a deer for a better hunt, for example, he or she dons the deer mask, dances the spirit of the deer accompanied by drums or rattles, and is able to communicate with that deer spirit more easily and fully on its own terms. But is the mask always necessary to affect change in the magic worker? Can change also be seen in the rest of the body without the use of a costume?

Some claim to be able to physically shape-shift, and I do believe that a certain amount of this is possible. Whether it's a material change in people, or their aura is so changed by what is happening to them, people do see a difference in others during deep attempts to shape-shift. Just prior to donning a Bast mask and channeling Her energies, others in the room saw my face change noticeably. I have also heard tales of shape-changing rituals that resulted in eye and hair colors being altered to a noticeable degree, people appearing to grow larger or smaller, and so on. But is this all glamourie and tricks of the candlelight?

Shape-shifting has long been claimed by both shamans and Witches, the latter being documented in numerous Inquisition reports of practitioners turning into cats, toads, stags, and other animals. There are also a few bits of testimony from that time that claim no outward change is seen in the Witches when they transform, so it could be the internal self-perceived change these accused Witches were testifying about. Likewise, when modern

Amazon Basin shamans are observed, nothing outward happens, but they claim to have become jaguars, birds, and so forth.

Perhaps what is happening is a misunderstanding of perception. The Amazon shaman is likcly dancing his animal inside himself during trance, and does not mean that his body literally transformed into a jaguar when he says he became one. The magic worker who is attempting to literally transform herself, however, may be manipulating the fabric of reality just enough to either project an illusion or glamourie around herself, or actually manipulating realty enough to affect some real physical changes.

We have seen examples in the first chapter of people who have been able to cause physical changes by using only metaphysical means. In the second chapter, we explored the fluidity of reality, further focusing on the fact that a person's will can alter the world. It is no stretch then to believe not only that shape-shifting occurs, but also that shamans and other magic workers are able to achieve this as part of their practices.

In my approximately twenty-five years of occult study, I have seen a lot of things that come pretty close to true shape-shifting, including statues that move, slight changes to other circle members during rituals hosting a deity, and assorted examples of friends giving themselves permanently changed physical features over time. Do I believe shape-shifting happens? Sure. Have I ever seen anyone turn into a cat like Harry Potter's Professor McGonagall? No. But I haven't seen a lot of things that I know can happen and do happen, so I'm not prepared to say it's impossible (and as we know from a previous chapter, nothing is truly impossible).

Another phenomenon that drew the attention of skeptics is the famous Oracle of Apollo at Delphi, also simply known as the Oracle of Delphi. Ancient accounts said that a woman sat in the temple on a stool over cracks in the floor, and vapors rose from the cracks that gave her prophetic abilities. Not having found these cracks in the temple floor, modern archaeologists scoffed at the notion of vision-inducing vapors and filed it away as a "myth." In the past few years, however, deep fissures have been discovered in the oil-producing stone under the temple that cross right under where the oracle would have been, and a team of scientists surmise that ethylene gas, which was once used as a euphoric anesthetic, was probably responsible for causing the oracle's visions.

The resulting visions of the oracle, while likely triggered by petrochemical fumes, were recorded to be strikingly accurate whatever their cause. And this is universally true of shamanic practices that use hallucinogens—the visions that come back to us through the shaman are extremely accurate when concrete details such as specific diseased organs or the activities of a remote person are described.

There are several examples, both modern and historic, of the shaman using mind-altering substances to enter the spirit world. According to medieval accounts ancient Witches used flying ointments to attend astral Sabbats, the ingredients including plants known to be hallucinogenic or poisonous such as monkshood and hellebore. Shamans of the Amazon rain forest use the well-known hallucinogen ayahuasca and other herbal concoctions to journey to the other planes where demons and helper spirits battle for the fate of people's souls. In North America, the native white datura bush and peyote cactus plants are used in a sacred way to travel and have visions.

Now, I'm certainly not advocating that everyone go off and take drugs to have a shamanic journey—I myself have never taken hallucinogenic drugs, nor do I drink alcohol—I am simply illustrating that the "inner" landscape found through altered states of consciousness is not merely a whimsical psychedelic head trip with no basis in our consensual physical reality. In fact, the entities encountered through these means appear strikingly similar to many different shamans, as illustrated by Michael Harner's adventures on the path to shamanism:

> I was now eager to solicit a professional opinion from the most supernaturally knowledgeable of the Indians, a blind shaman who had made many excursions into the spirit world with the aid of the *ayahuasca* drink.
>
> At first I told him only the highlights; thus, when I came to the dragon-like creatures, I skipped their arrival from space and only said, "There were these giant black animals, something like great bats, longer than the length of this house, who said that they were the true masters of the world." He stared up toward me with his sightless eyes and said with a grin, "Oh, they're always saying that. But they are only the Masters of Outer Darkness."
>
> He waved his hand casually toward the sky. I felt a chill along the lower part of my spine, for I had not yet told him that I had seen them, in my trance, coming from outer space.

> What I had experienced was already familiar to this barefoot, blind shaman. Known to him from his own explorations of the same hidden world into which I had ventured.

Harner also described parts of his vision to a Christian missionary couple, who found amazing similarities between some elements of what he saw and the Book of Revelation in the Bible, most of it specifically regarding the casting out of angels who fell to earth—Harner's "black dragon creatures from outer space." He sums up the discovery by saying, "The missionaries seemed to be awed by the fact that an atheistic anthropologist, by taking the drink of the 'witch doctors,' could apparently have revealed to him some of the same holy material in the Book of Revelation." Which naturally begs the question: Did John use psychotropics to receive this revelation or was it a naturally derived vision from an angel? I suppose we can never know the answer to that.

One way of using your body's natural drugs to alter your brain activity is to stimulate your endorphins through sex magic. We've all experienced that "drugged" state of bliss after achieving orgasm, which is body chemistry in action. Some magic workers use this climax and release to direct energy while engaged in sex, especially with the help of a sympathetic partner. Personally, I have other things on my mind besides working spells during intimacy, so I have not tried using orgasm as a cone of power as others have, but I do know that the euphoric time afterward has lent itself to some absolutely brilliant ideas and interesting trains of thought. Obviously, solo sex would be another way of harnessing this internal orgasmic energy and dreamy afterfeeling for completely undistracted workings and meditations, especially if you have a nonmagical partner or no partner at all.

It's interesting to note that one of the core trance postures advocated by Felicitas D. Goodman is that of the Lascaux "bird man" who is shown with an erect phallus. Some of the students experimenting with this posture experienced "base chakra" energy, or a tingling at the base of the spine or in their genitals, when they began meditating in the same posture shown in the cave drawing. Many stone and ceramic life-size phalluses have been found throughout Middle Eastern and Mediterranean archaeological digs as well, but we are forced to guess what they were used for. We may never know the depth to which sex magic was employed by ancient magic workers, but it makes sense to use this natural mind-altering experience to our advantage. Try it and see if it clicks with your methods and needs.

Dance is another age-old method of achieving that altered state of mind without drugs, and it's a method that knows no cultural boundaries as well. You don't even need to be a shaman to experience it—any kind of energetic dance can boost the body's endorphin level and produce a state of euphoria, from mild happiness to complete trance depending on the situation. For example, someone out for a night on the town with a loved one may find that dancing together makes her feel happy and in love, whereas someone down the street in a mosh pit finds himself doing things ordinarily thought of as foolish or dangerous, but in a state of frenzied euphoria he derives pleasure from the frenetic activity of crashing into the other "moshers" and diving headfirst into the crowd.

Aside from simply achieving a euphoric state through endorphins, dance can be part of the way humans interact and interpret the divine. Some shamans are described as "dancing" their power animal, even if their movements don't look much like a "dance" to the casual or unfamiliar observer. It's the dance of life, the dance of the animal or spirit translated through the human body, that the outside world sees.

Purposefully using dance and body movement to attain this altered state is a key way for the shaman to work alone, or for the priest/ess to achieve a powerful ritual for many participants. Starhawk's Spiral Dance, held every year in San Francisco, now has an attendance of well over a thousand people; the ritual has to be held in giant warehouse because of the demand. It's a lengthy ritual and spectacular enough, but when it comes time for the great spiral dance near the end, the energy becomes heady, jubilant, a bit chaotic, and certainly mind altering. Any Pagan who has been to a public ritual knows that the spiral dance is something hoped and waited for, and those who have been a part of one of these spirals knows what goes on in their head and body as they become part of the moving serpent of energy coiling its way into the center and back out again.

A famous example of using dance and movement to achieve an ecstatic bond with the divine is the whirling dervishes of the Sufi faith. Literally translating to "spinning doorway," the whirling dervish enters a trance state through the spinning of his or her body on its own axis and around other dervishes, which opens them up to the spirit of God. The hands are positioned, one facing up and the other palm down, to receive and direct the divine energy received from Allah as the ecstatic meditative state is reached while

The whirling dervish, lost in trance as he or she spins, directs Allah's energy from heaven toward the earth by bringing it down through the upturned right hand, through the body, and out through the left hand.

spinning to ritual music accompaniment. While I doubt that too many Sufi dervishes would call themselves shamans, they are achieving the desired altered state of consciousness through body movement and the use of music to contact divine energy.

If you wish to incorporate movement and dance into your practices, you certainly don't need lessons! Intuitive, natural dance is one of those things that anyone can do, and if no music is wanted or needed for a ritual, simple repeated movement to a rhythm instrument or a spoken chant is all that's required to achieve that altered state. You must let yourself turn inward completely, becoming one with the dance and the chant (if a chant is used), and you will soon forget to pay attention to what your body is doing. Your mind will wander out to that place of pure energy and access it easily for whatever working you're doing.

If a ritual like this is done with a group, you will likely need one person to "stay behind," probably the drummer or chant leader, to sense when the energy is right and bring the group back to focus it on the goal's completion. You'll also need to take care of practical matters such as moving all the furniture out of the way, avoiding tippy altars with candles that could cause a hazard, and ensuring the carpet has been vacuumed in advance to avoid mood-ruining shouts of "Ow! What did I just step on?" Stubbed toes and candle-burned hair are not exactly the kind of physical trials required for proper shamanic practice.

One practice that is a form of physical trial, and one that I've found to be very effective for deep inner workings, is that of the sweat lodge. Your body is subjected to intense moist heat, complete darkness, and reduced oxygen intake, resulting in anything from mild light-headedness to extremely deep journeys and visions. Through my own firsthand knowledge of the sweat lodge, I'd venture to say that the depth of the experience depends a good deal on the heat of the sweat, with the traits of the individual coming in second place. A sweat that's not hot enough produces little more than a friendly sauna experience, whereas a sweat so intense that you nearly lose consciousness will give you intense insights or even visions no matter how much of a skeptic you are.

While I certainly do not claim to be an expert on the subject, I have run sweat lodges for other people based on what I learned in Yosemite. To clarify a point, I am not of Indian ancestry (as far as I know—my mother was adopted) and do not claim to be the keeper of any ancient holy tradition; I simply have found the sweat lodge to be an excellent means to achieve an altered state of consciousness without the use of mind-altering drugs. Additionally, I would point anyone wishing to write me angry letters to the fact that the Native American sweat lodge is mirrored in the healing saunas and baths of Scandinavia, Europe, Asia, and the Mediterranean. According to the Asatru Folk Assembly, the sauna is sacred to the Birch Goddess and is viewed as part of their spiritual practices. True, it is probably the American Indian sweat lodge that is the most focused on attaining a religious experience, but you cannot emerge from a true Mediterranean *hamman* or Russian *bania* unchanged.

Further, according to my own experiences and interviews conducted by Mikkel Aaland in the 1970s, many Indians have no problem with non-Indians making and using their own sweat lodges, saying:

> I asked many Native Americans how they felt about this cultural loan. Most responses were positive, though a few had reservations. The Sioux leader of my sweat bath during the Sun Dance ceremony had one caution. "Sweat lodges are easy to make. You can pray to your own gods and take herbs that heal. But without a medicine man or spiritual leader, it is not an Indian sweat."

Black Elk wanted the ancient ways to be remembered by his brethren. His teachings in *The Sacred Pipe* and *Black Elk Speaks* makes it clear they were intended for all people— Indians and non-Indians.

This has been my experience as well, having been invited to Paiute sweats and Miwok roundhouse rituals without judgment, only acceptance, trust, and love. However, I was disappointed to see a woman on the television recently claiming that "only Indians can use the sweat lodge" in response to two deaths that took place in a sweat lodge near where I live. The news report made sure to point out that none of the participants was Indian, and the woman's further comments implied that it may have been divine retribution for whites daring to "steal" an Indian practice. Personally, I feel there is nothing wrong with constructing a simple blanket-covered dome and having a sweat in it as long as no one is claiming or pretending that it is an authentic Indian ceremony.

It should be noted that the mistakes made by the people who died were covering the entire lodge with plastic and burying the edges to make it airtight, and in making the sweat far too long (I have heard reports that it was supposed to last an incredible four hours). Obviously, someone in charge had no clue to what they were really doing and what might result, so again, be smart and get your facts straight if you decide to do a sweat, especially when you involve other people who may be harmed if you are careless.

Now that we have the lengthy disclaimer and explanation out of the way, allow me to tell you what happened to me during one Paiute sweat I attended. It was my first one, actually, and as we approached the lodge we were each handed a sprig of the local artemisia sage that's sacred to the Indians of California. We were told to breathe deeply in the sage if we ever felt too hot or thought we might faint, since it was to be a very hot sweat.

After we all entered, moving clockwise as we stooped and crawled toward our seats along the walls of the lodge, four red-hot rocks were laid in the central pit and the flap was closed to begin the first of four rounds. The stones sparkled and spat as the first drops of water hit them, releasing clouds of steam in the total blackness. I could hear the other participants around me shifting and breathing, and in the anonymity of the place I felt that we were all one, and all connected as part of a rainbow tribe in the sacred hoop of life.

The sweat continued, the flap being lifted about every fifteen or twenty minutes (it was difficult to tell how long it really was in that timeless place) to let fresh air in and allow the people who couldn't handle any more to leave. The light felt like an intrusion, but the cool air was like the breath of the Great Spirit keeping us all going. Four more large, glowing rocks were laid in each time, and the sweat continued. Several times I had to breathe the sage and sought out cool air along the bottom edge of the lodge with my hands, my lips feeling rubbery and my body drenched in sweat.

We sang sacred songs and talked about what we needed in our lives and what we wanted to get rid of. I could feel myself slipping away during the third round, and barely breathed out the words of the chants as they went along. Soon they seemed very far away and below me, but I suddenly felt quite alert and felt that light was somehow streaming into the lodge from above, making the steam visible. Before my eyes the steam coalesced into a dancing woman, all in white like a ghost. She did a two-step and turned around and around, holding out her arms to reveal a shawl with long fringe that moved as she danced. Soon I came back to myself and the flap was opened again. I stayed through the fourth round to the end of the sweat, but did not see the dancing woman again.

It was many years before I discovered who the woman was. One evening I was taking a very hot bath and closed my eyes, enjoying the steaming water. The dancing woman with the fringed shawl appeared again, and this time I recognized her as White Buffalo Woman—she has been with me ever since as a gentle guide filled with wisdom and perspective.

Building your own sweat lodge is not difficult, and filling it with willing participants and hot rocks is almost as easy, but there are some health dangers involved as well as ways of making the experience a spiritual one rather than simply a lot of sweat and steam. First, be sure that everyone who will be sweating is in reasonably good health and does not have mobility problems, claustrophobia, a heart condition, epilepsy, or any other condition that may cause the person pain, fainting, or even death. As I mentioned above, you can die inside a hot, airless sweat lodge if you are not careful and ignore your physical limitations. Your body is going through a lot of physical stress, not the least of which is hyperthermia, so do not go through a hot sweat if you have any questions about your body's ability to handle it.

Making the sweat a spiritual one does not mean simply singing Indian songs and repeating a few words of Lakota someone read on a Web site. You are going inside the womb of the Mother to be changed, or inside Turtle to emerge reborn into the fifth world. In the traditional Indian-style sweats I have attended, there are four rounds (times when the flap is closed), with four stones being placed in the central pit each time the flap is opened. Think how your group could use this format to reflect the directions, the seasons, different deities, or the individual needs of your group. You could also use three or five rounds or different numbers of stones if your group thinks it would fit better with what you want to do, but I don't recommend more than five rounds unless the sweat is not very hot, or you could run into heat stress trouble.

Choose your lodge location carefully—it should ideally be next to a stream, river, or pond so participants can jump into it when they're done with their sweat, but this isn't necessary, especially if the outside air is cool. The site should be level and free of any materials that could catch fire accidentally or injure your guests, and the fire pit should be lined with stones. If you're not near a stream, have two buckets of water nearby, one for fire safety and one to pour on the stones inside the lodge.

A note about the stones: Make absolutely certain that the stones you will be using do not contain any residual internal moisture. Otherwise, when heated until they glow red and then cooled suddenly when doused with water, they could explode. In my area, the local Indians know that the abundant native granite does not make a good sweat lodge stone because it tends to explode, and they use special volcanic rocks instead. To avoid potentially severe injuries, always heat and then douse your stones in advance to be sure of how they will behave inside a closed dome surrounded by people.

A simple traditional sweat lodge is relatively easy to construct with stout young willows, vines or rope to hold it together, and blankets to cover it completely.

Figure out the best place to put your lodge on the site, then sweep it clean and dig a smallish (eighteen- to twenty-four-inch diameter) central pit to hold the stones. Mark out a circle around this pit about fifteen feet in diameter and construct your sweat lodge dome by making a sort of upside-down basket. Use stout green willow branches or branches from any other tree that is tall, supple, and available nearby in quantity. Bury the larger end, curve the branch down so that it meets the ground on the opposite side, and bury the smaller end to make an arch about four and a half to five feet high. You can arrange the first two branches so that they lie north–south and east–west if you like, or use the cross-quarter directions to make your door face a particular direction, and tie them together where they cross at the top.

Continue adding more bent branch ribs until they are buried two to three feet apart at ground level and you have a dome shape. Leave one set of ribs a little wider apart for the door, which should face the river and fire pit. In my area, the door traditionally faces east, along with that of the Indian dance roundhouse and all traditional homes as well.

Now use more willow branches, grapevines, or other long and flexible materials to twine the arches together. You'll want to twist two strands around each main rib to hold it securely, placing these woven strands every couple of feet apart until you reach the top of the dome. Don't forget to leave one section open for the door! When you're done with the frame, you can use a tarp to cover the dome to keep extra steam inside (a tarp, unlike sheet plastic, still breathes), or you can simply cover the dome with lots of blankets in the traditional way. Keep layering on blankets evenly until you see no sunlight through the sides of the lodge, and remember to lay the blankets carefully to form an easily opened flap where the door is, using large safety pins to secure the flap to the top of the dome and clothespins to keep it shut if your flap blanket won't stay put. If you like, you can lay towels, sheets, rushes, or additional blankets on the floor where people will be sitting, especially if everyone will be nude. (Tip: You can often find inexpensive blankets and bed linens at your local thrift store.)

Decide in advance who will lead the sweat inside the lodge and who will stay outside to tend the fire and help with running it. The main priest or priestess should ideally have been to a sweat

SHAMANISM AND ECSTATIC WORSHIP · 83

before so he or she knows what to expect, and should be physically up to the job. The priest or priestess has the advantage of sitting next to the door flap, however, so will not be as affected as those sitting in the hottest spot opposite the door (make people aware of the temperature differences before they enter so they can choose where to sit). The fire tenders should be experienced at running a large, open fire safely; they will be the ones handling the red-hot stones as well.

As a practical note, decide in advance whether your sweat will be "skyclad" (nude) or clothed. If clothed, have people wear bathing suits or all-cotton tank tops and shorts to minimize any additional heat trapped against their bodies during the sweat. Also have them bring at least one towel (one for washing up afterward and an extra for sitting on if you're not providing a ground covering) and anything they might like to bring for sharing around the campfire afterward, such as musical instruments, snacks, stories, and so on. Before the sweat they should bathe, pray, and ideally fast for a minimum of several hours (if you're having it in the evening, a light breakfast but no more than liquids after that). But as with anything in this book, feel free to adapt these guidelines to your group's needs.

About an hour or more before the sweat is to begin, place your stones in the prepared outside fire pit (if you're doing four traditional rounds, you'll need sixteen grapefruit-size stones). Stack up the fire so that it will start easily and burn very hot, using about a third of your firewood. Start the fire and always have one of your tenders there to keep an eye on it and add more wood. You want a very hot fire, so keep adding wood as needed right up until the sweat begins. Check on your rocks, make sure they are bright red in color, and invite everyone to enter the lodge, purifying them before they go through the door.

Traditionally, people would be smudged and then given a sprig of artemisia sage, then they'd circle around the central pit from left to right as they entered. If you can't get the traditional California mugwort sage *(Artemisia douglasiana)*, I've found that the common nursery artemisia "Powis Castle" is an excellent substitute, being similar in fragrance and thus having the required cooling aroma needed when you're feeling too hot in the sweat lodge.

When everyone is seated and ready to begin, have the bucket of water and some kind of dipper (ladle, cup, shell, washed tin can, whatever) brought in and placed next to the HP/HPS, who enters last. Aromatic herbs like lavender, sage, or mugwort, or dried rose petals or other fragrant botanicals can be added to the water if desired (not traditional but nice). The stones are carefully brought inside the lodge and placed in the central pit (a shovel is probably the easiest tool to use for the job). The flap is closed, the HP/HPS may say a few words, especially to honor the stone people teachers in the center, a dipper full of water is sprinkled on the stones, and the sweat begins.

Generally, the flap is opened about every fifteen minutes (four rounds = an hour) to allow people to leave, to admit fresh air, and to receive four more red-hot stones for the next round. Those who leave during the sweat are not admitted back in once they are gone. Each round should focus on a different need, lesson, or the like, and the sweat should come full circle if possible when the last round is over. Of course, since you're not doing a traditional

Indian sweat you can run yours differently to fit the needs of your group—I'm just relating what I've learned over the years at traditional sweats as a model.

A couple of practical notes: Have people leave their eyeglasses and musical instruments outside. Glasses will fog up and don't do you much good in total darkness anyway, and instruments, especially drums, don't appreciate the moist atmosphere of a sweat lodge. You may wish to provide a basket lined with a towel outside the door for eyeglasses and put the fire tenders in charge of any valuables while the sweat is in progress.

When the last round is over, and the closing prayers have been said, have everyone leave by completing the circle around the lodge and go clockwise to the door. If your location is near a pool of water or creek, it feels absolutely terrific to plunge into the cold water and wash away all the heat and sweat. Even those who hadn't planned on getting into the water before the sweat will find themselves whooping and yelling as they splash about with joy and relief.

Another technique of both communing with the Great Spirit and achieving an altered state through physical hardship is the vision quest. Similar practices involving physical hardship to attain visions and messages from the divine may be seen in the Osirian mystery rituals of the ancient Egyptians and in the Sun Dance of the Native Americans.

In the vision quest, the seeker goes out into the wilderness alone, often for a certain number of days, and often while fasting and praying for a vision. This ceremony is usually part of a rite of passage, such as from childhood to adulthood, as part of shamanic training, or as a shaman seeking guidance for the group or for herself. It is also another example of a shamanic ritual that's usually thought of as a Native American practice but is found throughout the world, including Africa, Scandinavia, Australia, and Europe. It's even been theorized, based on the artifacts found with his tattooed body, that the famous "ice man" of the Alps, the fifty-three-hundred-year-old preserved human remains found inside a Tyrolean glacier, was on just such a vision quest when he died.

Obviously, if you wish to attempt a vision quest, you should at the very least notify someone responsible of where you are going, how long you will be gone, and when you should be expected to come back. This sort of common sense is also practiced by the traditional cultures that employ the vision quest as part of their spirituality, so there's nothing silly or shameful in keeping yourself safe. You don't have to tell anyone *why* you're going out; just make sure that if you get lost or injured, someone will know when and where to come and look for you. This is true especially if you plan on fasting and/or going into areas where dangerous animals such as bears or mountain lions might encounter you. All of this isn't to scare you off from doing a vision quest, however—such a quest is an excellent path to that vital one-to-one contact with the divine and provides a chance to separate from the mundane for a while, and have a deeply personal and meaningful religious experience.

Doing a vision quest isn't about meditating in your living room, it's about going out away from your daily life to seek wisdom and visions. Do it in a place of wilderness, going as far away from the city as possible so that you can be one with the earth and away from people and other distractions. This is about your relationship with the Great Spirit, and you need to be in that quiet place of beauty to hear some things that can't be heard anywhere else.

Something that you might encounter while on a vision quest is animal helper spirits. In a later chapter, there's a guided meditation I use to help people discover their helper spirit, animal or humanoid (or even plant), but these spirits can also spontaneously reveal themselves to you. I already knew who my animal helpers were when I went on a short morning-long vision quest, but other animals showed themselves to me in both solid physical form and as a fleeting glimpse that vanished before my eyes. Some were likely the spirits of that location rather than personal spirit helpers, and others were close relatives of my usual helpers, so it might have been a way of saying hello to me in that place.

That morning I got up before dawn, perhaps at 5 A.M., and drove to a local mountain peak that I had loved since moving near there as a child. I knew that the northernmost peak had been used ceremonially by the local Indians, and I could understand why— Mount Diablo is one of California's power points, there is no doubt in my mind. I parked in the lot and began walking up toward the Castle Rocks portion of the state park, a small basket containing only water and offerings in the crook of my arm. I had been to this spot before, not on any park map, and knew it was a special place.

The sky was growing lighter, and a fat full moon was getting lower on the western horizon. I found the flat bedrock slab at the top of the hill and sat down to rest, my leather moccasins and the hem of my wool cloak wet from the dew. I lay down and looked up at the sky, and at some point I fell asleep, then awoke just in time to see the sun just breaking over the rocky cliffs. I stood up, one hand stretched toward the rising sun and the other toward the setting moon, and I was sure that time had stopped, held in a perfect planetary balance. Birds began to sing as the sun warmed my face and dried my clothing. I left offerings at the four directions and tied a string of bird feathers into a nearby branch, prayers left to fly up to the Great Spirit.

I sat on the stone for several hours, and on that amazing morning I saw visions of bluebirds and a bobcat. Then the sun heated up the valley below enough that the nesting vultures began to swoop circles over me, their red, bald heads glowing in the sunlight and not more than fifteen feet above where I was sitting, just skimming the tops of the gnarled oak trees. The shadows grew shorter, the vultures became little more than specks up in the blue sky, and the moon was gone. I knew it was time to go home.

You may have found that many of the things discussed in this chapter involve personal contact with the divine. True, it is one of the primary functions of the shaman, but I have elected to handle this rather large subject in a separate chapter. Not all people using shamanic techniques become possessed or host a deity, and not all people who host a deity use shamanic techniques.

It is my opinion that shamanism, or at least skill in working with altered states of consciousness, is vital to the magic worker who wishes to advance beyond casting simple spells. Whether you believe in a higher power or not, sooner or later you must experience a reality outside of yourself to expand your horizons and perform such acts as psychic healing, skilled and accurate divination, Veilwork, or even simply being able to accurately read the energy of a group of people. Pretty much everything in this book is based on being able to achieve that altered or heightened state of consciousness, whether through meditation, ecstatic ritual techniques, perception of other planes of reality, or direct contact with a deity. Shamanic technique is at the core of being able to handle these more difficult workings, both for your own safety and for a successful result.

5

Fae Blood, Fae Magic

"If you will come with us, we will lead you into a country full of delights and sports."
—R. C. HOARE, ELIDOR AND THE GOLDEN BALL

"Every time a child says, 'I don't believe in fairies,' there is a fairy somewhere that falls down dead."

—SIR JAMES BARRIE, PETER PAN

"Those who have dealings with the fae are forever changed." —UNKNOWN

"Hey BillyJoe, I saw an Elf in the woods over yonder a few days ago."

"Um...what?"

"I swear it, sure as you're sittin' here with me. I sure do love livin' out here in the sticks where you can still see stuff like that."

"Um...right."

A CONVERSATION LIKE THIS MAY LEAD TO A NUMBER OF things, including a really great fantasy novel or a trip to the psychiatric ward. But our unnamed protagonist here wasn't imagining things—he spotted his neighbor Darlene picking berries at her favorite spot near his cabin. Darlene claims to be an Elf, and he has no reason to doubt her. She usually wears comfortable yet flowing clothes in earth tones, favors silver leaf-shaped jewelry, speaks to the birds (which appear to understand her), and simply exudes magic.

Lest you think that Darlene, the gentleman above, and this author have gone around the bend, there are many people today all over the world who claim to be Fae. And I have no reason to doubt them either. After all, what is the nature of reality? As Michael Harner said, in his metaphysical classic *The Way of the Shaman*:

> Dragons, griffins, and other animals that would be considered "mythical" by us in the Ordinary State of Consciousness (OSC) are "real" in the Shamanic State of Consciousness (SSC). "Fantasy" can be said to be a term applied by a person in the OSC to what is experienced in the SSC. Conversely, a person in the SSC may perceive the experiences of the OSC to be illusory in SSC terms. Both are right, as viewed from their own particular states of consciousness.

Thus, building on the previous chapters regarding altered states of consciousness and the fluid nature of reality, it is entirely plausible that "fantasy" creatures and beings not only exist "somewhere," they also exist right here in this "reality" as well.

In a 2001 article in *Fate* magazine, author Cara Des'tai describes these people who understand themselves to be elves, dragons, and other kinds of what most people would call "mythological" creatures:

> Who and what are these "otherkin" and "fey"? They are people who know that their souls are not completely human, usually having distinct memories of living in another plane of existence in other forms, and often with a longing to return across the gossamer veil that separates this world from their home. They can usually work magic easily, especially workings like "glamour" (disguise) spells. Those rare few who are sensitive enough to see their true forms see these folk as beings of legend, including elves, dragons, felinoids, dwarves, wood nymphs, merfolks, satyrs, and others.
>
> [Fey] tell of commonly forgetting to eat or sleep, speaking an unknown but distinct language as a toddler, being able to shape shift, and in one case actually being able to breathe underwater for short periods of time with no ill effects.

So we have individuals claiming to be "beings of legend" and beyond, with a feeling of differentness about them. I have encountered some of these individuals, and although I cannot see a complete astral overlay of some fantastical creature, I do sense an "otherness" or "separateness," something magical and quite nonhuman about them. It's a sort of mental silver shimmer, not one you see with the eyes (at least for me), and a feeling of internal and innate powerful magic, as if part of them is made of magic.

And that is what they feel as well—that they are not human (to varying degrees) and that they are made up of magic...that they are magical beings, at least in part. Rather than think of the Fae as only fleetingly glimpsed little pixies who hang out in the garden, however, this chapter deals primarily with people who view their soul as not completely human and working with those otherworldly magics.

A quick set of definitions: In this chapter we are dealing with the idea of "elf" not as one of Santa's little toymakers, but rather as they are seen in classic mythologies—the Tuatha de Danaan of the Celts or the Alfaer of the Germanic tribes. Tolkien, taking many of his ideas of fantastic creatures and their languages from ancient cultures, also depicted the elves as tall, slender, attractive humanoid beings who are both magical and otherworldly as well as earthy and organic. As long as you look at the older classical myths, other stereotypes hold true as well—dwarves are short of stature and appreciate things like gems, metalwork, and mining; dragons love to hoard things and can be easily provoked; satyrs are dramatically earthy and sexual; angels are the messengers of the divine as well as their sword-carrying source of justice; and so on.

The Internet, being the instant means of worldwide communication, has produced a large Fae or Otherkin community with many message lists, bulletin boards, newsgroups, and so on. So it's not just individuals walking around with ideas that could easily put them in the nuthouse—there are hundreds, perhaps thousands of people who feel that they are Otherkin, and many of these find the online community after their own self-discovery, not the other way around.

Back in about 1996, a message was posted to several news-groups, including alt.pagan and alt.magick. The "Elven Nation Manifesto" outlined who the elves are as a people and suggested ways to forcibly open the Veil to allow more magic into this world. Typical replies to this message, which numbered well over a hundred, included "so that's what I am" and "it's about time someone recognized us."

Since then, the online Otherkin community has matured and grown. Groups have come and gone, split and formed. Many who initially identified themselves as elven now see other traits in themselves, such as dragon, angelic, nymph, satyr, lycanthrope, and so on.

Of course, it should be said that not all of these people truly possess the "otherness," and some are plainly "wannabes," but I don't feel I can judge a person's innermost being (can you?), and the wannabes do find the game tiresome eventually and wander off. A parallel can be drawn here with the Pagan community, which sees influxes of naive youths after films like *The Craft* and *Practical Magic*. They find out it's not like Hollywood and move on after a while.

Outside the Internet—inside of which reality can be tenuous and connections to others temporal—real physical communities of people who identify themselves as Otherkin are beginning to form. Somehow these folk are gravitating toward each other, or perhaps to a location, such as where ley lines intersect or where a spot in the Veil is thinner. According to a researcher in Canada, the small communities or Fae groups number about fifteen members each or less, usually in rural areas away from city pollution. One of these smaller groups is the Silver Elves, located in rural California and mentioned in Margot Adler's *Drawing Down the Moon*.

Alternately, some Fae love city life, finding beauty in the weeds of vacant lots and viewing it as an opportunity to spread a little magic into the heart of the mundane world. The first nationwide "glamourbomb" campaign, in 1999, featured ideas such as arranging pennies in complex sigils on sidewalks and placing notes with sayings like "your wings are real" inside fantasy novels at the library.

I suppose in a way it doesn't really matter if the Fae are who they believe they are—it's an internal judgment, and as long as it doesn't interfere with the person's ability to function in society, we should not be quick to dismiss the notion and scoff. After all, many psychiatric professionals still say things like "do you consider yourself to be a witch?" when doing an evaluation, and much of the mainstream media still thinks we're nuts, using phrases like *self-proclaimed witch*, or *Jane Doe claims to be a witch*. Naturally, you never see things like *self-proclaimed Christian* or *Jane Doe claims to be a Jew* in the newspaper. But enough about my pet peeves.

Personally, I do believe that there is something "other" about them, and their magic feels different to me than other kinds of energies. There appears to be a wide overlap between what I would consider "Fae magics" and what many Witches do as part of their magical practice and exploration. For the purposes of this chapter, however, I have set aside some ideas and techniques as "Fae" because they read that way to me, and in my experiences on some Fae/Otherkin mailing lists certain things seemed to be discussed more often or were completely unique to that community. Obviously, you may hold a different opinion as to what is Fae and what isn't, so just roll with it and enjoy the information presented here.

One of the more lighthearted things I've encountered, as mentioned above, is "glamourbombs." These were so named because glamourie is probably the most common form of Fae magic, and that magic was delivered to the unsuspecting mundane world with the intent of changing it. Many ideas were devised for the original 1999 campaign besides those previously discussed; there are whole Web sites devoted to glamourbomb ideas and techniques. The main idea behind it all is to introduce some unexpected magic to the unaware citizen, keeping in mind the idea that "those who deal with the Fae are forever changed" and that more magic will enter the world when more people are aware of it. Naturally, in light of recent world events and because *bombing* connotates violence, the campaign is now being called just "glamouring."

Other ways that the Fae have been working to get more magic into the mundane world is through Veilwork. As we saw in a previous chapter, most Witches understand that the Veil exists and acts as some kind of barrier between the world we're all familiar with and any number of spirit and/or astral realms. However, I've found that it's primarily the Fae who actively work *with* the Veil as opposed to working *around* it. I don't know if it's the case, but it appears to me through anecdotal evidence that many Fae have an easier time perceiving and handling whatever "stuff" makes up the Veil between the worlds.

Another aspect of the Veil is as a barrier to the lands of Faerie. There are many old tales of people wandering in the woods who become lost or who find a strange path that leads them to the

Kingdom of Faerie, complete with Oberon and Titania and the rest of the attending host of pixies, brownies, gnomes, and so on. If the people ever find their way out again, time is very different and many years may have passed in the outside world, much to their dismay and grief. Alternately, as we see in the famous book *The Lion, the Witch, and the Wardrobe* by C. S. Lewis, hours may pass in Faerie while mere seconds have transpired in the mundane world.

I read an anecdote on the Internet that described how a group of young people recently tried to find a way into Faerie on Midsummer Eve. They cast a circle, magically readied themselves as best they knew how, then called upon the circle's protection and started off to find the way in. Most of the group almost immediately got lost (I'm sure the dark night didn't help things out), but one person spotted a path she had not seen before. She was very familiar with this local hiking area, and was surprised to see it, being even more surprised that the path appeared to be very faintly luminous. A chill went up her spine as she began to follow the path. After about an hour of walking, the path became more obscure and she became completely lost and confused, worried that her friends would be frantic to find her. Eventually she found her way back and, like Lucy in the aforementioned book, found that only a few minutes had passed while it seemed to her that she had been gone for quite some time.

This kind of manipulation of the Veil and glamourie are classic Fae magics. Glamourie is any kind of magic that makes you appear as you are not, such as making yourself seem more beautiful, being invisible or receding into the background, appearing to be someone else, and so on. One elven woman I know uses glamourie to mess with people's heads for fun:

> I've dyed my hair bright red, then used glamour to make it
> look its usual brown color. It's great fun to watch and see
> which of my coworkers don't see anything, which ones see
> right through the glamour, and which ones peer at me re-
> peatedly because they know something's not quite right but
> can't figure out what it is.

I've used what is either invisibility or some variation of "don't notice me" glamour many times, hitting upon it before I realized what was happening. The first time I did it by instinct—I was sitting up on a big rock by the creek on our land and a group of neighbors and their visiting relatives came noisily trooping down the hill and crossed the creek about seventy-five feet from where I was sitting. I wanted to be left alone, so I just froze in place and sort of mentally said "you don't see me...you don't see me..." while seeing myself as part of the moss-covered rock. Imagine my surprise and delight when the whole group passed right by me, one woman even looking directly at the rock, and no one noticed that I was there.

In another example, I was sitting at the bottom of a large red-wood tree playing a little lap harp while waiting for some friends to show up. A young deer walked over the little rise in front of me and I froze, repeating the same sort of "you don't see me...I am part of this tree..." mantra to myself lest I startle it. The deer walked by barely three feet away from me, innocently nibbling plants near my feet and looking around cautiously for danger. Sensing none, it slowly continued past and meandered back up into the forest.

More mundanely, I have used the same mantra and feeling of pulling myself into the background when on somewhat questionable city streets and crowds of people have looked right past me. After the first incident by the creek, I tried experimenting to see if I had imagined it, and scared some of my friends and family out of their wits when I suddenly appeared next to them (and was duly chastised for sneaking up on them like that). It appears to work quite well—try it and see if this technique works for you.

Choose a public place, such as a park, and sit down where people are passing by. You may use the base of a tree, a park bench, or even try it in plain sight in the middle of a lawn. Notice how many people see you sitting there, perhaps smiling, nodding politely, or simply making eye contact with you.

Get comfortable, calm yourself, ground and center, and sit perfectly still. Picture an aura or mist around yourself that matches the background you're sitting against, pulling it backward through yourself so that you become "flat" against the bench or tree. You may feel a slight tingling at the front of your body as the energy moves away from it toward your spine. Alternately, you may try to form a colored mist around your body to act as camouflage, such as the color of the grass if you're sitting on a lawn. Within this withdrawn state, repeat a mantra of "you do not see me" or something similar, being careful not to project this thought outward— this defeats the purpose. You are trying to become invisible to the casual passerby.

Draw the aura backward to lay behind yourself during an invisibility glamour working.

When you feel you have achieved this withdrawn state to its fullest, hold it and begin to take a mental tally of how many people notice you there. When you start to become fatigued, let your normal auric state return gently and see if more people notice you there once again.

Now that we've covered the two most common kinds of what I consider to be Fae magic, let's follow the luminous and obscure path a little farther. We dealt with Veilwork primarily in that chapter devoted to it, but there are things surrounding the Veil that the Fae have been working with as well. One of these things is the role of the "Guardian," and while some may scoff and say the name is borrowed from a Mercedes Lackey novel, it is also found in western ceremonial magic traditions and quite descriptive for what Fae and other experienced magic workers have been handling, perhaps since magic was discovered by the first shamanic proto-humans.

Guardians are sort of the "Cosmic Veil Police." They find a trouble spot, whether it's a spontaneous hole in the Veil that's allowing troublesome entities through or a vortex created by inexperienced people playing about with magic they don't understand or can't handle. Guardians generally sense the problem themselves or are called by someone who knows they can help. Most work within driving distance of where they live so they can go to the site physically and clean it up, but some do all their work on the astral plane.

Cleanup methods are as varied as the problems that can crop up, whether it's as simple as helping a noisome discarnate spirit find its way back across the Veil or a major rip in the Veil acting as a "hellmouth" (to use an apt term from *Buffy the Vampire Slayer*). Some techniques may involve more conventional and familiar physical items, like a buried "witch bottle" filled with bent pins, razor blades, and urine, but most ways of dealing with these events are primarily astral or energy-derived, such as "stitching" the rip closed with energy threads in the form of a sigil. And of course the individual may have a unique specialty that can be employed more effectively in these situations, such as the astral sword of an angelic, the raw coercive power of a lycanthrope, or the purity of a unicorn.

One important magic technique that I came across several

years ago and recently rediscovered in Sandra Ingerman's book *Medicine for the Earth* is that of unique energy sigils. Ingerman tells her readers: "When you understand the power of symbol, let a symbol of your creator that you can use for meditation form in your mind's eye. This will allow your own unconscious to begin merging with your higher power."

Beyond simply being used to meditate on, however, your symbol or sigil can be used for very powerful magic workings. If you already have a sigil in mind for this, be sure it's unique to you alone and not an ankh or cross or something else commonly used by others. This is yours alone, for your use, just as a shaman would use his own personal power song while doing a healing or other working.

If you don't have a sigil that you use magically in this way already, seek one out through meditation or through a deep guided meditation facilitated by another experienced worker. Mine was shown to me on the astral by another magic worker. It may also come to you in a dream or as a spontaneous gift from your deity. However your sigil comes to you, be sure you can retrieve it instantly, making a drawing if necessary to trigger your memory when you first find it, but don't rely on this drawing forever. If you are consistently forgetting your own sigil, it obviously doesn't have the necessary power to be very useful and may not accurately reflect your personal energies.

But what can be done with this sigil? As mentioned above, you can use it to repair a rip in the Veil, to heal another, to put up protective wards, to signal to others on the astral if they know what it looks like (think Bat Signal!), and so on. This is a symbolic visual

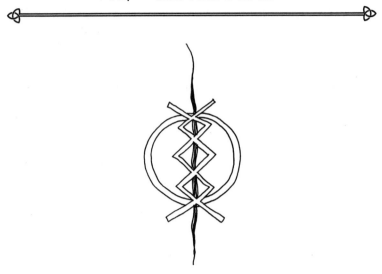

An energy sigil can be used to repair a tear in the Veil.

representation of your own spirit energy, so use the sigil as an organized and concentrated "essence of you" in magical workings. If you or someone you're working with is visually impaired, or the visual sigil is just not working for you, feel free to use another type of cue in the same way, such as a sound, word, motion, and so on. Just make sure it accurately reflects your own personal energy signature.

Let's assume for the moment that your sigil is a visual one, and that you see it in your mind's eye and on the astral as a glowing symbol. Mine is a triangular sort of thing that's hard to describe, and it looks like it's made of bright green lines of light. Get comfy with seeing your sigil in this way. Now use the same color of light to draw a more complicated sigil, such as a pentacle, seal of Solomon, septagram, and so on. Try using different colors of light and see how different they feel—try red light for a powerful protection sigil, blue or green light for healing . . . you get the idea.

If you're using sound or another alternate energy signature, try changing it around to work with more complicated sounds, motions, or the like. You can also change the pitch of your sound or speed of your gesture just as I would change the color of my light depending on the need.

When you're comfortable working with more complicated sigils, it's time to try creating a simple energy matrix. A matrix can be used to hold a door open in the Veil, to help hold in the spirit of a dying person, to connect and bond people together, or even to do planetary workings, as we will see below.

Use a symbol you're familiar with, such as a pentagram or your own sigil if it has "corners," and visualize it in the colored light. Using the pentagram as an example, attach the points of the star

Anchor an energy sigil to a location that needs to be marked, protected, guarded, or otherwise tended by your energy while you are away.

to the floor or wall in front of you, allowing the center to float freely. When it's secured, try lifting and moving the points, then reattaching them. See what that feels like for a moment, then release the matrix and let it dissipate. Try a different matrix in a different color (or several colors at once), experiment with it, and release it. Try putting it across a doorway as a protective ward and see what happens. You might even try this in a public place and see how many people unconsciously veer around your matrix or become attracted toward it.

Of course, larger and more intense workings can be done with more complex sigils, especially when others are working with you and helping to weave the light or even serving as anchor points (more about this later). Once you've gotten the hang of working with basic energy sigils, you're ready to try using them to create things like anchor points between two locations, portals through the Veil, permanent energy signatures in a specific location, and vortexes to return discarnates to where they belong.

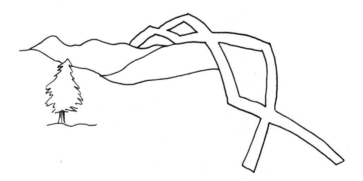

Energy sigils can be stretched between physical or astral distances, connecting people or objects magically.

Obviously, these are all potentially dangerous workings, and could cause harm to yourself, to others, and to the Veil—do not attempt these workings or anything like them if you are not 150 percent confident in your ability to do them. Also, I cannot stress enough the importance of working with others of your same caliber to double- and triple-check exactly what's happening. Sometimes when you're in the middle of it all, you don't see the stuff sneaking past your peripheral vision or can't see the forest for the trees, so to speak. There is no shame in asking others to help you perform a difficult working! Brain surgeons and army generals don't work alone either, and this is the level of seriousness you're working with, too. This is not playtime—you are manipulating the fabric of the universe as well as dealing with beings from other realms, and not all of those beings are very nice things to allow through the Veil. They will eat you for lunch if you don't know what you're doing.

Now, having freaked you out enough for the time being, here's a little more of a description of the techniques I mentioned above—it should give you an idea of what you can accomplish with the energy matrix. To form anchor points between locations or people, simply stretch the sigil out between them, anchoring them equally for balance (make sure you have everyone's permission before attempting this sort of linkage!).

The Veil portal is more tricky, so some careful experimentation would seem to be in order to determine what works best. In sacred space and with others present to help you, open a small hole/door/portal in the Veil (one that can be easily monitored and closed quickly if need be). Use a matrix to hold the door open so that you

A sphere or vortex can be used to help a person cross the Veil or return a discarnate entity to the other side.

are using your energy to maintain the matrix rather than the door. You can also make a tunnel from the door in the Veil down to the earth to ground any wayward energy or spirits that might come through, or direct any energy raised in your ritual through the Veil.

This leads into using a sigil or matrix to help a discarnate to cross over. Naturally, use your best judgment here so that you're helping the situation, not making it worse by trapping on the other side someone or something that doesn't belong there. Work in a group and get a second (or third, or fourth...) opinion before starting. When you're sure about what you're doing, use the symbol formed of light around the being, and cause the symbol/ sigil/matrix to spin faster and faster in a ball or whirling cone of light to contain the discarnate inside. When everyone is ready, open a portal in the Veil and push the being through to the other side with the still-spinning matrix of light. An obvious application of this technique would be to resolve a violent haunting or to help a lost soul cross over.

Another way of using this whirling energy vortex is as a portal through the Veil for you or your group. An example of such a use is described here by Arathan, an Elven man I know from the Internet:

> A friend of mine has a sort of cairn in his backyard (this sounds awful, backyard cairn) but it's true (he lives in a rural area) and there is a large stone underground that makes a small bump on the ground and it seems to be the "center" of the cairn. My friend and his brother began to make the energy exchange and to make it go in a circle pattern, and this enabled me to get a clearer look at things around in the spirit world.

He goes on to describe a childlike pink Faerie whom he saw while in the middle of this vortex, which apparently enabled whoever was in the center of it and sitting on the cairn to see into that realm. He also described to me a spherical portal that he and his fiancée created as a way of contacting Faerie energies, one of the unusual characteristics being that it was distinctly warmer inside the sphere than outside, where it was a cold, windy day. This temperature difference has been noted in old folktales of Faerie rings, as well. Obviously, there are many other ways of using a charged vortex, sphere, or other energy structure as a portal to other planes when you desire contact or workings outside a deep trance state.

Permanent energy signatures can be as permanent as you like, meaning that they can last for the duration of a ritual or for eternity (be smart about that last one!); it depends on your needs. The idea here, however, is to create a freestanding sigil or matrix of energy that does not need your attention to survive, but can be lifted and dispersed by your will when you're done with it. Create a ritual that can be done in the location where the sigil is to remain. The ritual should also use things personal to you, such as your power song if you have one, perhaps some physical items like hair or an offering of sage or tobacco, or simply your presence and force of will if that's enough to make the energy stay put. (Sit! Stay! Good boy, energy!) You may also choose to draw the sigil or matrix out in salt, tobacco, chalk, or another appropriate material for the location. (Don't use tobacco in a garden, by the way, since it can spread tobacco mosaic virus and kill some flowers and vegetables.)

Attach the sigil to the physical location with visualization and concentration, then carefully detach your energy force from it, leaving some energy behind to power the sigil without your direct attention. In other words, make your sculpture but save the rest of your clay for later. To draw the sigil back up, simply reattach your energy to it and let it dissipate. You may also choose to draw the energy back into yourself, but unless you know who or what has been in contact with it, you may not want to do that and risk bringing foreign things into yourself.

These examples of personal energy work with sigils should get you started—I'm sure you can imagine other possibilities for this kind of work. For example, one group in particular, the Order of ChAOS, has been using sigils and energy work to open the chakras of the earth, in anticipation of the birth of the new aeon.

On the Order of ChAOS Web site, several very complex and theatrical rituals are shown in which the initiates receive body piercings at each of their chakra points; then these piercings are fitted with a small ring through which threads are woven, forming pentagrams, septagrams, and so on, for the appropriate magical purposes. Obviously this kind of ritual takes incredible willpower, dedication, and magical strength! The rituals for resonating with the earth chakras also involve this chakra weaving technique. If you're interested in finding out more, I recommend their Web site, which has loads of interesting photos of their rituals and other information including ways of participating translocally (www.crossroads.wild.net.au/vision.htm).

Another form of weaving threads in relation to magic is purely on the astral. One night, many years ago, during some ritual before my altar (I honestly have no idea what the ritual was about now), I suddenly saw shimmering, pale, rainbow threads stretching out before me, going off into the black distance so that I could not see their end. I opened my eyes and they were still faintly there in the candlelight, then closed my eyes again and there they were, shining brightly. I gingerly reached out and touched them, stroking the threads with my fingers—they were like soft cotton yarn. It struck me that these were the Threads of the great Loom, and that each shimmering strand was the life of myself and those around me; the farther away from my own thread they were, the less connection I had to them.

I have felt for some time that each person has a unique energy signature and that signature is a different color. I have never seen what most people consider to be an aura, but I have connected a color to a person's energy, so either I'm right on the mark and it reflects what the Threads show, or I'm perceiving the Threads in those colors to match my inner feelings. In any event, I have successfully worked with these Threads and used them to get an idea of what's coming up on a large scale that affects many people.

Some time in about 1999, I began to see what I call a "Great Tangle" out at the edge of where I can perceive the Threads, out in the misty darkness. It was a mass of Threads all snarled together in a big lump; then the Threads came out on the other side, but there were fewer of them. As time advanced, I saw the Tangle coming closer and closer to myself, until, shortly before September 2001, I perceived that we were right on the leading edge of it. I don't think I need to spell out what happened then.

About a year after I started seeing these Threads, I stumbled upon a series of fantasy novels that almost exactly describe what I have experienced. I was amazed and shocked by this, then I spotted a bit of an e-mail to a Fae newsgroup describing Threads. I contacted the poster and, sure enough, she sees almost exactly the same thing I see. That verification sure felt great! It's yet another example of why I think working in groups, or at least getting another point of view on a working, is incredibly valuable for verification and as a "reality check."

Obviously, the primary working that can be done with Threads is manipulating the actions of others. Something that should be just as obvious is that this wanders over into that "harm none" gray area of casting spells on other people to manipulate them. Just as with any magic workings that affect other people, be extremely judicious in how you use this kind of magic. If you are able to see the Threads and choose to use them in your work, they function as you would expect something like this to act—to be closer to a person, move his Thread over toward yours. If you wish to avoid a person, move her Thread away.

In the past, I have used Threads to contact someone whom I was unable to get a hold of in any other way during a minor emergency, and to ensure that I would be able to meet a particular celebrity in order to pass along some important information to him. By identifying which Threads belong to which people and moving them closer to or away from your own, you increase the chances that your paths will cross (or that you will be able to avoid the person).

Identification is trial and error, especially for people that you don't know very well. As you handle the Threads, think of the person and see which ones "sing" to you. Stroke each likely Thread and continue thinking of that person, and through intuition you will eventually be able to narrow it down or be pretty sure which one is the right one. As I said, I work in colors, so it's perhaps a bit easier for me to simply find the right-colored Threads and go from there. There's no right or wrong way to do this—it's all intuition in the end, so simply experiment and see what works best for you.

Of course, all this assumes that you are working within the usual linear time stream as represented by the Threads. Time is a liquid thing, especially for Fae and Fae magics, as we have seen above. Many magic workers, especially those who have practiced for a long time and/or those who are interested in quantum theory, are also using the idea of nonlinear time in their workings.

Think of it this way: One-dimensional existence would be strictly linear with no area. A two-dimensional existence would have an area but no mass, like a flat paper doll or a television image. A three-dimensional existence, like the one we're all familiar with, includes depth and mass so that we can move up, down, sideways, diagonally, or any way we wish in any direction. Time is the fourth dimension—which we are also familiar with, of course—though we usually perceive time as only going in one direction. But it is simply another dimension that we can move around in if we understand how to do this.

The realm of Faerie doesn't quite take as much stock in linear time as does the mundane world, and time can move more slowly or more quickly there. They understand that it's a matter of sliding along the time stream in any direction, and while it may be difficult to go upstream rather than to "go with the flow" of time, it is possible with a powerful enough motor on your boat and the will to do it. It's also possible to jump sideways over to other time streams, just as you would go through the Veil to jump to other planes of existence.

As with any working that involves altering the fabric of reality, extreme forethought and caution should be used when altering the time stream and thus the subsequent course of events. Some current quantum theories involving the time stream include the idea of branching event conclusions (any choice results in a branch,

2ND DIMENSION   3RD DIMENSION   TIME
(4TH DIMENSION)

so any situation creates many multiple branches of parallel universes), time travel by jumping between alternate universes, and endless time travel event loops in the same universe.

Working with the time stream in a moral sense is a lot like working with Threads—you may be able to go back in time astrally and alter something, but it should only be done if it does not impose your will upon someone else. It also takes a considerable amount of willpower, skill, and magical strength to be able to attempt something on this level, not to mention possible divine intervention. Speaking of divine intervention, as with any complex working that involves the very fabric and nature of reality, don't be surprised if you are brought up short by a divine force—it may indicate that you were about to mess up something important on a cosmic scale and needed to be prevented from doing so.

I hope this chapter has opened some doors to you as a practitioner, making you aware of some interesting things other magic workers have been doing, and giving you new insights, techniques, and ideas for your own work. Fae magics are perhaps the most wild and unfamiliar kinds of workings for many traditional Witches and other Pagans who may have been used to the tamer methods of simple candle and herb magics. There is nothing wrong with good old-fashioned spell casting, certainly! But my hope in writing this book, and this chapter especially, is that experienced magic workers can look beyond what they're used to—the physical, the familiar, the tradition-based training—and explore things they never imagined to exist or that they didn't realize they could tap into.

6

When the Spirit Moves You

"There is danger in writing these things in books. The danger is for those who know little, but who believe they have power. We have no power: We are only vessels."

—WAKEYATU-TA-SHOKA-EE-HAMBALAY

"There absolutely has to be a purpose to call [the Spirits]. They are not toys."

—SHAKMAH WINDDRUM

"Just because they're dead doesn't mean they're right."

—OZ

"CHANNELING" HAS BEEN IN VOGUE FOR PROBABLY TWENTY years or so in the new age arena, with strange and apparently mystical messages being given to average people by aliens, archangels, deities, and the dead. When you read some of these "alien/ angel/spirit messages," however, you have to pause and wonder just how lucrative this business of channeling must be for those who frequent the talk-show and convention circuit, and what reference material they're using to come up with some of these "messages." Not to say that they're all charlatans, certainly, but I personally think the signal-to-noise ratio is pretty iffy.

Even farther back there was the "medium" or "spiritualist" craze of the nineteenth century, which, when you remove the aliens and archangels, looked and sounded suspiciously like the aforementioned channeling craze but with the added excitement of table tapping and other noises, plus ectoplasm and other physical manifestations. It was the overabundance of charlatan "mediums" that caused many countries to write laws against this kind of activity, many of which are still on the books today and affect modern Pagans.

But what about the honest seeker who encounters a deity unexpectedly, or the priestess that has the Goddess drawn down into her during a ritual? Direct work with the divine is not only a part of most Craft and shamanic traditions, it's expected, one of the main traits that differentiates Pagans from "organized religion," which uses a hierarchy of special men to do this for us. Most Witches and magic workers are very familiar with receiving messages from the divine and speaking with their favorite deities. This can be through prayer, a guided meditation, daily devotionals, or even unexpected and spontaneous visitations.

Once while I was camping alone at a festival, I was thinking about my then current love life and was frustrated because I wasn't sure what to do. I had just broken up with my boyfriend of five years and felt adrift, not sure if I should go with a guy I liked but had just met a few months prior, or if I should sort of feel out the local Pagan scene for possibilities. I was walking through the forest, wishing the Goddess would give me a sign, when the forest disappeared and was replaced by what I can only describe as a movie of the same bit of forest. Everything looked the same, but somehow distant and flat and unreal. A few yards in front of me on the path appeared a woman, whom I knew instantly was the Goddess. She was very tall and fair with very long blond hair, and her face was not there—it was a blank, blurred-out oval where a face should be. I knew immediately it was Aphrodite.

She stepped to one side, and there behind her stood the man I liked but didn't know that well. I dropped to my knees, crying with wonder and thanks, and when I looked up again the forest had returned to normal. After the festival I started getting to know that guy better; we were married about a year later. We have been married for what seems like a seamless eternity, and we still feel like we're on our honeymoon. My husband is a true soul mate and gift from Aphrodite herself!

I suppose even the thickest heads can still receive visions of the divine, but I believe that if we are open to it, these kinds of spontaneous visitations and messages are more easily received and are more likely to occur. If you're trying to visit your friend to deliver a gift, it's much easier to walk through an open door than a closed and locked one.

Opening up to these energies and possibilities are not just something you do when in circle or at a ritual. If you want to live your religion in your daily life, you need to retrain yourself to be ready at any time to see and experience the unexpected. I say "retrain" because children are already open to this, and it's only through years of people telling them "there's no such thing as magic" (a nod to Harry Potter's Uncle Vernon there) and the mundane world closing in on them as they become older that they lose this freedom. But more on that in the chapter on intuition later in this book.

Every day, try to remind yourself that magic is real, and that whatever God/dess you are closest to is always right there beside you. Daily exercises to open up your psychic and Spirit awareness are also a good way to get those juices flowing. In a place where you can meditate undisturbed for about fifteen minutes, ground and center yourself. Breathe deeply and be still for about a minute. Ask for the ability to be still, to listen, to see the gifts of the divine. Picture your mind or your third eye opening up wide, and extend your awareness or aura out away from you, using it like a thousand little fingers to touch the world around you on the astral. Hold this for a few minutes, but do not fatigue yourself—if you feel strained, pull your aura back. Rest, breathe deeply, and slowly return to your waking self. Make notes of what you experienced, and do this exercise as often as possible.

You could also wear a pendant or some other jewelry to remind yourself to be more open to magic; charged jewelry adds a lot to the effect. But be aware that things may present themselves to you in sudden and unexpected ways the more open you become, the more you are able to see the magic and the spirits of things around you. Alternately, if you find that you are being bothered by spirits who follow you home because you're the only one who can see them, a piece of charged jewelry to help ward them off may be in order.

Outside random and spontaneous encounters, your most usual workings will likely be direct contact initiated by you in the context of a ritual. It is in this space that you will have the safety and freedom to work the most closely with the divine. A lengthy essay titled *On Deity Assumption* was presented as part of the annual Leadership Institute at Covenant of the Goddess' "MerryMeet" in 1995. In it, the authors categorize hosting a deity in four degrees of intensity: Enhancement (speaking about, reciting); Inspiration (speaking for); Integration (speaking as); and Possession (silent, while He or She speaks). This really helps illustrate the levels of depth that are encountered while the Priest or Priestess deals directly with a God or Goddess. The closer you get, however, the more you will need the help of others. Even the most experienced Witches and magic workers do need the help of other people in the sacred space to help ground, protect, and guide you.

M. Macha NightMare explains this a bit further:

> I think the supersensitive, or untrained and unaccompanied/unassisted can risk danger if they leave their own personae. I think they can have trouble getting all the way back, and this leaves them vulnerable to "this world" dangers, like car accidents, things that result from being unaware, from being "not there." In other words, they can get in over their heads.
>
> They are also at risk of deluding themselves. There's the danger of self-aggrandizement, advancing personal agendas in the name of a deity, faking, kidding yourself and/or others. Fantasy and desire can be misinterpreted as fact.

When asked about the kinds of problems people can have while hosting a deity or spirit, another experienced priestess named Oz had this to say:

> Several negative results may occur. A person can become possessed, which can lead to a weakened will, psychological and physical problems. A person's life can be destroyed from this. I have seen this more than once.
>
> Many people today believe that keeping positive thoughts and working "White Light" will prevent this, but unfortunately that is not always the case. Even without actual possession, a person may develop an obsession or become deluded or addicted. States can occur that are similar to chemical dependency.
>
> Because I began this work young and without adequate training, some of my early experiences had negative effects on my body, and I find that some of my organs are weakened because of that. Some of my most powerful early experiences left me physically ill, and had lasting effects.
>
> The best way to avoid these problems is to avoid working alone. Get training. Find a teacher. Test your guides. Stay involved in some kind of magickal group, Temple, or Lodge. Time will usually tell if your guides are benevolent, but only an experienced teacher can help you keep a balance between your astral life and your physical life.

So while you may feel knowledgeable and indestructible, it is not wise to push the envelope without experienced people present. It is a good idea, however, to become more familiar with the sensation of direct contact with the divine and speak with the deity you wish to work more closely with. Before your first attempt to host a deity or channel a spirit, you should get to know that deity very well and understand his or her needs before allowing the spirit to enter you. You should carefully examine the feeling of the deity's energy so that you can differentiate it from your own if it is having trouble leaving and you need to consciously separate from it. If you are inexperienced and will be working with other priest/esses during the rite, make sure they understand what is expected of them, know how to handle the situation in case of a problem, and know what the energies of the deity or spirit feel like in advance.

As mentioned above, another thing to look out for is too much overlay of what you want and expect during the ritual. The purpose of hosting a deity is to give that deity a vehicle through which he or she may communicate with others, not to control the deity or improve your public image.

M. Macha NightMare had this amusing observation about hosting spirits and divine beings, which she calls "aspecting":

> In my experience, when an aspecting is "true" and "pure," the host is not recognizable as the person you know. The person's speech patterns, accent, gestures, way of walking and moving—all are changed. All are different from what you know that person to be. Deities don't, in my experience, talk in pop psychology terms. They don't talk like Valley girls or Boston Brahmins or bayou country folk, and They don't talk

in fake Elizabeth English, using lots of "thees" and "thous." They do, however, speak in the language of the people who summoned Them.

Although I have a lot of trouble letting go of myself and I'm overly self conscious when I try to allow Bast through me, I definitely feel as though She aligns with who I am and easily speaks through me in English, not ancient Egyptian. What would be the point in that? No one seeking Her words of wisdom would be able to understand them!

It's more of an overlay for me, not a total uncontrolled possession complete with glossolalia and fainting as you sometimes see in various kinds of rituals. Of course, the degree to which the deity takes possession of a person's body varies, depending on the individual's ability and/or willingness to yield to the spirit in question. Your mileage may vary, as they say, so don't expect the same results between people or even between sessions with the same person.

Perhaps you think you're ready to be a channel for a deity or spirit and would like to try it. You could simply call the deity to you and give it a whirl, but this would be as foolhardy as trying to drive on the freeway with no driver's training. You must truly be ready, with the right preparations and experience, or you could find yourself having some of the problems mentioned earlier in this chapter.

When you feel you are truly ready to allow a deity or spirit to work through you, you must prepare for the experience carefully and with purpose, especially the first time you attempt it. Oz had lots of great advice when I asked for her opinion on what sorts of things people should do to prepare:

Get as much training as you can. Find classes that teach psychic development. Keep yourself psychologically healthy, including seeking therapy when you need it. Learn to do banishing and cleansing work. Study psychic self-defense. Keep in constant communication about your work with a teacher or a magickal group.

Keep yourself physically healthy as well. Powerful psychic work can put a strain on the bodily systems. If you use fasting or anything that challenges your body, follow these times with rest and nurturing for yourself.

Maintain a positive relationship with all the deities and spiritual entities you work with. Treat them with utmost courtesy. Most ancient cultures maintained regular practices of giving offering to deity, both as a way of honoring and of maintaining a healthy exchange of energy. Ask your deities how you can return energy to them, whether through service, practice, offerings, or all of these.

Maintain a respectful attitude toward your spiritual beings, but do not consider them infallible. They may be deities, but remember that their communications to you are always filtered through your own mind. Question what you believe you hear. Ask for clarification and verification. Do not follow "channeled" communications blindly. Keep up a dialogue with your beings, and be sure they are aware of your own needs and feelings. Do not assume they know and understand everything about you. Do not be afraid to express fear, doubt, pain, sadness, and other so-called negative emotions. Keeping these suppressed can create blocks.

Remain open to joy, and remember that many beings in other worlds have a great sense of humor. Practice love in all dimensions.

You may have a familiar deity or spirit whom you wish to work with, or you may not have a patron/matron deity at all but wish to act as a priest/ess for your group's benefit, or for your own personal guidance. If you're not sure or don't have one, use a deep guided meditation to discover who would like to work with you. Go in with no preconceived notions or expectations of what you will find—more often than not it will be a total surprise, sometimes a baffling one, but almost universally a pleasant experience.

Have an experienced magic worker, shaman, or priest/ess guide you into a deep meditation to help you find this deity or spirit. One meditation I use is to have the person astrally walk out into a pleasant place she likes, such as a desert, grassy plain, deep forest, or other location. Once there, she sees a tiny figure way off on the horizon. As they approach each other, it gradually becomes more clear who or what this figure is, and the scenery can change to reflect the place this being or animal or spirit comes from if it makes sense to do that—you don't see too many dolphins in the desert, for example. Ask the being what its name is, thank him or her for coming to you, and give it a gift of some kind (don't worry—

During the guided meditation to find your guide, it will appear on the horizon, and as the guide approaches you will be able to better discern who or what it is.

something will materialize in your hand, or you can give physical affection, or what have you).

Return to the ritual space and describe everything you experienced with your helper(s) for additional observations. Of course, if you feel comfortable doing so, you can attempt this contact by yourself since it's not really that difficult, but it works much better to have a partner verbally guiding you from outside so that you can devote all your attention to what you're seeing and not worry about the mundane stuff or otherwise get distracted.

Whatever deity or spirit you wish to work with, make sure you study everything you can about him or her. Does the deity have a favorite color? A favorite food? Is the deity associated with other things you can bring into the ritual space with you, such as certain stones, animals, or tools? Surround yourself with all these things, and ground and center yourself. As you think on each aspect of this deity, perhaps wearing the deity's favorite color, reciting one of his or her stories or songs, and so on, notice what changes you sense in the room and inside yourself. Eat the deity's favorite food and honor him or her with poetry and songs, fondle an associated stone or item, wear some jewelry with the deity's image on it... just let the deity come and "hang out" for a while so you can become more familiar with his or her unique energies and whims. Become so familiar with the deity that it takes no effort to tell when he or she is near, and when it's time for the ritual, make sure your helpers are in tune with this entity as well. Also be sure they know when to help usher the spirit back out with appropriate wording that you've agreed upon in advance or that's so obvious

While hosting a deity, you will feel yourself astrally growing larger as the energy surrounds you and merges with your own energy field.

even those who are possessed could find their way back accordingly.

When you're ready for your first attempt, purify yourself by washing and anointing yourself carefully. Set up your sacred space as usual and place images of this deity on the main altar. If you're working with Bast, make the altar cloth green. If you're calling Hecate, place a cauldron there. You get the idea. An important aspect of ritual that many people don't utilize enough is fragrance—use an incense and/or oil attuned to that deity, especially when invoking him or her into yourself.

When we did mask work and invocations in my Egyptian group, one of the priestesses would kneel before the person and hold up a bowl of incense, fanning the smoke toward him as she said, "Great _____, please come into your priest now and let us all learn from your wisdom," or similar words. Perhaps it's because the Egyptian Netjeru in particular favor fragrance, but that step always added to the depth and immediacy of the deity's entrance.

Allow yourself to relax and resonate with the familiar energy signature of the deity you've been working with. You will feel yourself filling up somehow, becoming taller and larger with the deity's presence. You may also feel a tingling sensation or begin to perspire, feel a tightening in your gut, a temperature difference in yourself or the room, a sudden adrenaline rush or sudden calming, or a feeling of deep love wash over you that may bring you to tears. Try to take this on slowly at first until you are used to the unfamiliar sensations, and allow yourself and your concerns to recede to the back of whatever consciousness is in your mind. Take a moment, with your eyes closed, to enjoy the feeling and let the deity come forth however it is manifest. Then begin your working if you are doing this for the benefit of your group.

You may not remember much or anything of this "close encounter," as many of the people I asked said to me. Again, it depends on the depth to which you go—light trance may yield vivid memories, but complete surrender may leave you with a complete blank when it's over. Personally, I think that unless you're absolutely 200 percent certain that you're working with the actual deity and not some spirit masquerading about, and until you've done this for a few years, you should not attempt more than a light or moderate trance within this shared consciousness in case there's unexpected trouble. The same goes for having helpers nearby— they are there to ensure your safety.

During a ritual in which the other participants will be working with the deity within your body, you may be asked unexpectedly for blessings or words of wisdom. If you are still partially in control, allow yourself to recede and let the deity speak through you. It's hard when you're nervous and want everything to go perfectly, especially during a larger public ritual, but the deity knows what it's doing. Let him or her guide your actions, let spontaneity produce beauty and magic, and open yourself up to trusting that everything will turn out fine.

I attended a wonderful NROOGD ritual some years back in Berkeley where a friend of mine was to be invoked with Brigid. She was very nervous when the day arrived because she wanted the ritual to go well, and she wasn't sure what to expect since she had never attempted to host a deity so deeply before. The choir sang, the lights were extinguished, and she emerged from the back hall led by two attendants, the crown of candles on her head the only light in the room. She moved with grace and beauty in the pure white Irish linen gown (I'm proud to say I made it for her) and truly looked as regal as only the Goddess can look. She alit like a flower petal on the throne provided for her, and one by one the people went up to her for blessings. Her face seemed lit from within, her movements were poetry, her voice was like song, and you could feel the power radiating from Brigid sitting there in that room. Later, my friend said she didn't remember anything after the point at which the Goddess was invoked into her, and was surprised to find that wax from the candle crown had dripped all over her during the long ritual—she hadn't felt it touch her skin, and she was not harmed from the hot wax in the least. I think it's safe to say that this is a good example of a truly deep and powerful aspecting/hosting.

When I hosted Bast for the first time I retained most of my own faculties, but was still guided by Her during the course of the ritual for the benefit of others. Things before and during the ritual would pop into my head, and they all turned out to be terrific ideas that the other participants really loved. For part of the ritual I did a hands-on healing of each person, starting at their head and sweeping my hands down them to the floor where I would release the "junk" into the Earth. As this part of the ritual progressed, I became much more intuitive and could easily tell what parts of each person needed the most healing. I felt consciously nudged and guided by Bast, and had to keep reminding myself to let things happen as they would and not be such a control freak about everything. When it was over, I felt part of Her inside me still . . . or perhaps I learned to recognize that part that was always there. I felt terrific.

As you see in this example, the priest/ess is healed during these kinds of rituals, too, something that's also true of Reiki or any other system where you are opening yourself up to pure deity energy and channeling it through yourself. You should not emerge drained and weak from a session with your deity—you should be full of spirit energy and well-being from your encounter. Possible negative side effects include light-headedness and confusion, which are easily remedied by taking the time to ground yourself properly after the deity has left you.

Touching again on what I mentioned above, sometimes you might choose to continue hosting that spirit or deity (on a *much* lighter level) for a long period of time, especially if there is some-

It is possible to project your consciousness into other beings to gain their perspective and literally see through their eyes.

thing in particular you're working on. Oz tells me that she has "carried the presence of a Goddess in my body for as long as several months." If you find this too difficult or taxing to attempt, or simply need easy access to this deity for a period of time but don't need constant direct contact, you could try using a spirit guide to act as an intermediary. Many magic workers have spirit guides with whom they work closely anyway, so that might be an easier way for you to connect to the spirit realms and in turn connect to a particular deity.

Another way of connecting with spirits and deities is to flip around your ideas of hosting and become the spirit that enters someone else. As Oz explains, "In deep ritual and meditative states, I have entered the 'body' of a deity. I view this like entering a current of energy or a mass of thought form. In this state, I perceive mental, emotional and spiritual impressions derived from that deity, angel, or spirit."

One other way of being the spirit that another hosts is in the practice that many shamans employ of seeing through an animal's eyes. If you've ever seen the movie *Beastmaster*, it's something like the lead character does with his hawk—in a meditative state you project yourself inside the mind of the animal (or person) and see through his or her eyes, and even interact with others if the possession is deep enough. Obviously, use extreme discretion for this working and do not violate the will of another, or there will be a nasty karmic price to pay—as I'm sure you're aware.

Complete spirit possession, in which you are not in control of the situation or your faculties, is a technique of communication and communion used by some groups. Some shamanistic and ecstatic practices, such as the Afro-Caribbean paths (including Voudoun, Santería, Umbanda, and Candomble) use complete possession as part of their ritual experience. In each case, those possessed are never left alone and are carefully watched after by others at the ritual so that they don't come to any harm. As M. Macha NightMare sums it up, "Possession is something only safely experienced within the context of a community and in the company of experienced people who are not themselves possessed at the time."

Houngan Aboudja, a Voudoun practitioner I spoke to while writing this book, gave me some terrific insights into what happens to one who is ridden by the spirits. He confirmed that while many people are fully possessed by a spirit in that tradition's rituals and remember nothing later, there are times that lesser degrees of control are needed by the spirit and thus the person does remember at least some of what happens.

When a person is fully possessed, however, the attendants not only help prevent the person from injuring him- or herself, but also act as assistants to the spirit riding him or her. As Aboudja tells me, "Those who are trained to attend the spirit do whatever is needed—they get their clothes or tools, machete, bottle, food, et cetera. They may translate for the spirits, transcribe for them if needed, and so on."

So that's the dual aspect of ecstatic/hosting worship (of any tradition) that must be considered by everyone present, especially by the clergy members who are not being possessed and who are attending the one who is. First, make sure the person hosting the spirit is safe, and second, attend to the needs of the spirit within that person's body during the course of the ritual. If your group is small and the ritual is an intimate one for your group alone, you can probably have other group members take care of these needs as they arise. If you are going to be doing a relatively public ritual involving spirit hosting/possession/aspecting/riding/your-favorite-term-here, you will need at least one very experienced assistant who knows exactly what to expect and what needs to happen, or at least two trained attendants who can help the person and the spirit before, during, and after the ritual.

When the hosting part of the ritual is over, make sure the person can return to herself in whatever way she needs to do this. If she needs to return to a back room that's dark and quiet, get her there and make sure this departure is written into the ritual. If the "devoking" will be done as part of the ritual in the main room, be sure the attendants know how to do this properly, perhaps having everyone involved practice this as best they can beforehand, and be ready to help the person ground herself if necessary when the spirit leaves her. You may find that the person will be hungry, or thirsty, or tired, or full of energy, or she needs to urinate, or she may be light-headed... each hosting can be very different, especially between different people and different deities.

For example, here is an anecdote from Oz regarding some difficulties she had with Pele: "She had a very difficult time entering my body, and each working left me completely physically exhausted. She gradually learned to tone down Her vibrational energy to work with my presence and my psychic and physical limits. She explained this was partly due to the different constitution between

my Anglo-Saxon makeup and the Polynesian makeup that She is used to."

Only experience will ultimately guide you so that you can handle any type of hosting, yours or someone else's, with confidence and a successful result. While it can be somewhat dangerous, especially if the person is not prepared properly, spirit hosting is also extremely rewarding in many ways. If you and your group are ready, it is probably the best way to experience deities, loas, spirits, or other entities on a very "close-up and personal" basis. It will be moving, magical, and life changing for everyone involved.

7

Trust Your Intuition

"Imagination is more important than knowledge."
—*ALBERT EINSTEIN*

"Doing Witchcraft without intuition is like driving blindfolded." —*M. MACHA NIGHTMARE*

ONCE, I WENT TO A TERRIFIC WORKSHOP ON BASIC PSYCHIC ability. I've never considered myself particularly psychic in the usual terms—able to read minds or tarot cards, knowing when someone dies, being able to tell which card has the wavy lines on it . . . I stink at all that. So I figured, what the hey, maybe I'll pick something up, and went to the class.

It turned out the class was less on "how to read minds" and more on "how to trust your intuition." The teacher encouraged us to say what we saw, no matter how strange it sounded. In one exercise on reading another person, we took turns holding the other person's hands, closed our eyes, and just started saying whatever popped into our heads. The other woman's turn was first, and it almost seemed like she was trying too hard—she said very general things that could apply to anyone (a trick telephone psychics use) and even said I was pregnant (I wasn't and had no plans to be).

When my turn came, I was nervous. I held her hands, closed my eyes, and centered myself. The first thing I sensed was some kind of energy disruption in her lower back and said so. She replied that she has chronic pain in her lower back and has to take medication for it. Surprised and somewhat pleased with myself for picking up on that, I continued.

I kept coming back to a crown of dark red stones, and I couldn't fathom what that was all about. I finally said to her, feeling rather silly, "I see a crown of...I think garnets on your head for some reason." She stared at me for a moment, then said, "Do you know that when I do healing work I visualize a crown of gems on my head, and I take the gems I need off it to heal the person?" Now it was my turn to stare. That changed my opinion that "I'm not psychic" forever, let me tell you.

Since then, I've sort of relearned some of what I trusted as a girl. I've always felt energies, but in the stifling atmosphere of school bullies and a divorced household, some things fell by the wayside in the interest of daily survival. Magic and psychic abilities can be somewhat temporal and delicate things—the less they're used, the more you start to think they were never really there to begin with.

I asked M. Macha NightMare her thoughts as to why adults seem to have such problems trusting their natural intuition. She replied: "Because we've become so steeped in the rational. Things that can't be touched, quantified, measured, weighed, are not considered to exist. They are imagination, delusion, hallucination, whatever." And of course she's absolutely right. Just as military boot camp takes great pains to tear recruits down and remold them into good little soldiers, most schools and teachers take great pains to emphasize the physical world, statistics, memorization of dates and numbers, mathematics, and so on while forcing students to conform to standards and tests, often while wearing school uniforms. This ignores individuality, creativity, and the natural ability of children to dream and fantasize. Today's students spend more time at school and on homework than they do at play and with their families—it's boot camp for the "real" world of consensual reality, which crushes the magic right out of most kids. There's no room for magic in the mundane "muggle" world.

So how do we get it all back? Years and years of magic training and relearning may be needed to counteract the years and years of propaganda and unlearning that life throws at our children. For some, it may never be regained. Others may have been lucky enough to have had encouraging parents or a strong enough will to ignore some of the antimagic conditioning; they may be okay. The critical period appears to be between about six and fourteen, before which a child's imagination is encouraged and she learns nursery stories and legends, and after which she is strong enough to resist simply believing what she is told and feel the pull of magic. It is this middle period where schooling seeks to weed out the "strange" children and force them to conform to the needs of the material world at large, where natural intuition is most in danger of being buried so deeply it may never see the light of day again.

Learning to trust your feelings, your intuition, your "sixth sense" is not easy if you were one of those children. The sensitive child, the creative child, the daydreamer, the story creator, the child who could once see Faeries and dragons—it is this "inner child" (sorry to use such a worn term, but it's apt) that we must reclaim. The path is not easy or quick for most, but the even the longest walk begins with one step. Trusting yourself is the path to take.

For me, "psychicness" is simply sensing energy flows and patterns, something I can do with some aptitude, and having the trust

You may perceive "hot spots" of illness or pain in a person's body as fuzzy spots, different colors, spikes in their aura, tangled knots, or in other ways.

in myself to believe what I experience. Through experience, I've found that where I'm most skilled is in sensing a person's body energies, especially detecting trouble spots as in the case of chronic pain or sensing the general energy dynamics of a small group of people.

But this confidence has only come through years of forcing myself to trust what I experience and, more importantly, working with others to confirm or deny what I'm feeling. It takes a lot (at least for me) to say something that I think may be the wrong answer. It probably stems from the carrots-and-sticks of school days and fear of peer ridicule. But whatever the reason, I still have a hard time doing psychic exercises with others and reporting what I see for fear of being wrong or, worse, thought of as less competent than other Witches. If you have these kinds of self-esteem and confidence issues, too, I'm sure you understand what I mean.

Again, only repeated reassurance will add to your confidence and help you find what you're best at. Find some people you trust who have a modicum of psychic ability and try doing some basic exercises. Even if some of your answers are consistently wrong, they're still beneficial and will guide you toward your "specialty." As they say in the software industry, "It's not a bug, it's a feature!"

Another way to help learn some skills and gain confidence may be to merge with your patron/matron deity, as discussed in the prior chapter. The results may not be fully yours, but you will likely learn how to recognize things such as energy patterns or symbolic clues that show up in your head with the help of your far more experienced deity along for the ride.

This technique has worked very well for me, because my primary deity is Bast, a tremendous healing goddess. As mentioned previously, during a ritual that I was HPSing, I hosted Bast and did a hands-on healing and cleansing of everyone in my Temple. Beforehand I figured that I'd just run my hands from their heads to their feet and then give the "bad stuff" to the Earth. But through Bast's eyes, or hands, I could easily sense what people needed in the way of healing and felt their trouble energy spots as if they were painted on their bodies in glitter. My hands began to tingle; then the tingling worked its way up my arms until I couldn't bear it any longer and had to do a longer discharge into the Earth after each healing to be rid of it. What I experienced was confirmed later as I spoke to each person separately after the ritual and asked about certain things I'd seen. Now I can draw on that memory of what I felt at the time and I feel more confident and strong about what I'm experiencing now.

I think it's no accident that my matron deity is Bast and my primary psychic skills are hands-on healing and mentally seeing different aspects of a person's physical body. If you feel a bit lost when it comes to your intuitive skills, think of who your primary deity is and see if he or she can guide you. Do a ritual of discovery and have your deity lead you to what you sense best. You can also try merging with your deity and see if you pick up anything new or see a new avenue to follow. If you're very confident with your own personal skills, I'll bet they match pretty well with the deity you're closest to.

That's another way of gaining confidence in your intuition and abilities. As discussed previously, there are many ways to channel or unite with the divine. Assuming you do feel that link to one or more deities, and knowing that you are a channel for that Spirit, trust in that divinity to help you in your workings. I'm not talking about working *with* it as a separate partner—I mean work *through* it as it works through you. Become one with the deity, even in a small way, and allow that bit of spirit to flow through you. You can be assured that what you're seeing is real when you're guided by the divinity within you.

If you're not confident about your natural psychic abilities, start with some simple exercises to gain confidence and stretch your mental muscles. There are many to be found in various books, but I always like to use the simple technique of stilling and centering myself, closing my eyes, and letting my awareness wander until something "pings" in my brain. When you're comfortable with this technique, set a purpose for yourself in these wanderings, such as seeing what a friend is doing many miles away. While you're still learning to trust yourself, you can call the friend in advance and arrange for him or her to be doing something specific (but secret) at a certain time, then try to "fly" over there and report on what you saw. Even if it's completely wrong, keep trying, remembering to relax and turn off the analytical part of your brain so the intuitive part can do its thing. Report everything you see to your friend, no matter how silly or unlikely it sounds (sometimes tricky friends might try to do something strange to throw you off), and you might surprise both of you.

This is also the basis of what used to be called extra-sensory perception (ESP) but is now fashionable to call "remote viewing." The U.S. government conducted remote viewing experiments for many years, and has reportedly only recently discontinued these experiments, with program veterans forming their own civilian organizations to continue learning and teaching remote viewing. They claim that anyone can learn how to do it, and I believe anyone has the *potential* to learn how, but in my opinion only people who can learn to trust their intuition are able to skillfully see what's happening many miles away using only their mind's eye.

Continuing with your exercises, remember to keep a detailed journal of everything that happens, both accurate and incorrect. Make plenty of notes to yourself, writing down near misses (your friend was playing a video game rather than watching TV), similar circumstances (your friend's next-door neighbor was in the swimming pool instead of your friend), and possible explanations for complete misses (the event did occur, but some time prior to or later than when you saw it). Remember to ask your friend to keep a log, too, and record anything that originally was a miss but was either remembered later or actually occurred later—time is not necessarily linear or synchronized between physical reality and the astral plane.

Ignore complete misses for the time being and focus on the hits to gain insight and confidence. It's likely that some of the hits will be accompanied by feelings of "that's silly" or "I know that can't be what's really happening so I'm going to ignore that." I remember the feeling I got when I saw that crown of jewels. At first I discounted the image as impossible because it had no relation to my own experiences, but it kept coming back, and when I finally pushed away my feelings of "that can't be right" and checked with the other woman we were both surprised by how right it was. Looking back, I remember the deep intuitive feeling that it was

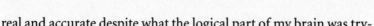

real and accurate despite what the logical part of my brain was trying to tell me—that's the feeling you want to capture in your work.

It may be different for everyone, but I get a good old-fashioned "gut feeling" when doing intuitive work—and I'm sure the cliché must have come from somewhere, right? I feel a sort of dark fuzziness somewhere in my stomach area when I get those intuitive buzzes, as well as snap flashes of intuition, sort of along the lines of "your first answer is the right one." If I want to know where the cat is, usually the first place that flashes into my head immediately upon asking the question is where I'll find him. I've noticed these two kinds of intuitive feeling when I'm working—the quick visionary flash and the deeper darker gut feeling that is less visual. What do you experience when you get an intuitive feeling? Is it visual or more of a "knowing" feeling? Remember to write down everything you experience and review your journal from time to time.

Another possible barricade to your intuition is internal barriers and shields. Many intuitives, especially naturally gifted empaths, have put up mental shields to help protect themselves from the daily barrage of other people's emotions. If you're especially gifted in this area, you may not even know you've created this shield, or may be afraid to let it down based on past experiences. If you're not sure, take some time to examine yourself and see if this is the case. When doing the exercises mentioned in this chapter, make sure you're working alone in the room and that the friend you're working with is alone, too, at least when you're starting to let the shields down and explore outside yourself.

An internal barrier we all have is that of disbelief, and for some

A person may or may not realize that they regularly shield themselves. Shields are often used by natural empaths to block out the overwhelming emotions of crowds.

people this can manifest itself inside as a real shield that needs to be dropped when you work. But as M. Macha NightMare says, "I believe that you don't necessarily check your brains at the edge of a circle. You need to lighten up on the analyzing part of your brain *during* but not afterward when you're trying to figure out what's been going on." The same goes for psychic/intuitive work—drop the shields and the analytical voice in your brain that says "this isn't real" while you're working, but then use it to your advantage later when reviewing your exercise journal and analyzing what's working for you and what isn't.

It should be noted, however, that while analyzing the results of an experiment or ritual or other event, you should be careful not to overanalyze it. It's easy to explain away something as "coincidence" or "the candlelight must have distorted what I saw" or worst of all, "I only imagined that . . . it's too silly or ridiculous to be true." You can be your own worst enemy when doing intuitive work! This comes from all those years of being trained to function analytically while ignoring or suppressing your intuition. Remind yourself constantly to keep an open mind, especially when trying to analyze the results of a psychic experiment, or it defeats the whole purpose of the experiment. It can be a delicate balancing act between using logic to find answers and pushing away the very magic you're trying to work with.

The more you learn to trust yourself and what you're seeing, the farther you can go with intuitive workings. Some organizations use trained remote viewers to foresee disaster and terrorist attacks with some measure of accuracy (even within the psychic community, many people disagree on what a realistic "hit percentage" is). The farther you go, the more individual the exercises need to be, so you'll have to be your own teacher for the most part unless you can find a very skilled and attentive teacher who can help train you. If you can't find a teacher, examine many different kinds of "advanced ESP" books and see which exercises work well for you and the types of skills you're trying to hone. In any event, make sure you work with at least one other person, preferably multiple people or a magical group to do "reality checks" on your progress. It doesn't do any good to try training solo, start down a path filled with inaccuracies, then find out later that you have to start over again and retrain yourself to recognize when you really have a "hit."

As in any form of training, you are likely to hit plateaus, and you will simply need to practice, practice, practice to become more skilled and get over that hump to the next level. Anyone who has learned to play a musical instrument understands this to be true—you start with scales and finger exercises, then learn some simple songs, then learn harder songs, and eventually—if you work hard enough and have the natural aptitude for it—you can become a virtuoso. But on the path to expertise, all musicians hit plateaus where no matter how hard they try a certain piece of music can't be played without mistakes, or a certain fingering trips them up every time. You may encounter a similar plateau, where you can't get better than a certain percentage of accuracy, or you find yourself unable to penetrate a certain location with remote viewing skills, and so on.

Sometimes the solution is to try a seemingly unrelated exercise, which can open up new avenues you may not have known existed. Any intuitive work, even if it seems to be backtracking or unrelated to the plateau you're trying to get past, is useful training and may help you understand what the problem is or give you a new perspective from which to approach it.

It should also be noted that if one path is not working for you, maybe you're on the wrong path. It sounds obvious, but it's true— if Gardnerian Wicca isn't helping your intuition grow, try shamanic Wicca. If shamanism isn't working, try Gardnerian Wicca, or OTO, or Reclaiming Tradition, or Metista, or Kemetic, or Greek Reconstructionism, or Asatru, or any number of other traditions that emphasize and use intuition to work magic. Work within your own tradition first (assuming you have one), but don't be afraid to journey onward if need be to find a method or teacher that works best for you if your current path isn't getting you where you want to go.

Aside from total reliance on intuition, some people also work through a spirit or deity for their remote viewing information. For example, famous psychic Sylvia Browne uses a spirit named Francine to gather much of her information, and allows the spirit to speak through her during many readings. Of course, you still must maintain a certain amount of intuitive ability to be able to contact these beings and receive messages through them. It's simply an example of another way to gather "psychic" information during a working.

Intuition is at the heart of any in-depth magical working, especially if you're a Pagan community elder/shaman/priest/priestess/ what-have-you, who will be expected to monitor a ritual's energy, contact spirits or deities, fix something when it's not going as expected, perform a healing ceremony, do work on the astral, or any number of other workings that require the use of your mental abilities.

I believe we can always use more exercises to increase our confidence in our intuition. This excludes, naturally, those who are overconfident to the point that they "no longer need" checks and balances, breezing into a ritual or convention and "telling it how it is" to the exclusion of the readings of everyone else present. You know who these people are, I'm sure. They may or may not be more accurate than anyone else, but they're convinced they've always got it right. I'll applaud their victory in the battle of trusting their intuitions, but they're also on the other end of the pendulum as to why anyone doing psychic work needs to work with at least one other person for reality checks.

Learn to trust yourself, but don't get cocky and develop a superiority complex about your skills. There's always someone more skilled than you, and there's always someone less skilled than you, so can you afford to make yourself look like a fool or a braggart? "It is better to remain silent and be thought the fool than to open one's mouth and remove all doubt." I love that saying, even if I ignore it too often. This does not mean you shouldn't say something if you honestly sense trouble, or if you think you see something others don't appear to notice, or if you're picking up on something so far off in left field it will sound silly to say it. All I'm getting at is that unwarranted overconfidence can be as bad as little or no confidence. Use your head, be modest, act with grace, and remember that your goal is to help others, not to make yourself seem more powerful than someone else.

Intuitive work is perhaps one of the most gossamer and difficult things a priest/ess can attempt, depending on the circumstances. Sometimes the magic "clue-by-four" is so obvious that even your oblivious rock-headed uncle picks up on it. Whatever the case, your own ability to sense unseen forces, energies, magics, and be-

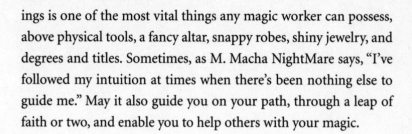

ings is one of the most vital things any magic worker can possess, above physical tools, a fancy altar, snappy robes, shiny jewelry, and degrees and titles. Sometimes, as M. Macha NightMare says, "I've followed my intuition at times when there's been nothing else to guide me." May it also guide you on your path, through a leap of faith or two, and enable you to help others with your magic.

8

Group Dynamics and Energy Flow

*"I think the thing I like the most about Festivals is
that they are a great legal high."* —GREY CAT

*"I remember well one year when these words could
be heard in Pagan circles from California to New
York: 'We are an old people. We are a new people.
We are the same people, stronger than before.' That
summer it was as though we were all remembering
something together."* —OZ

*We are the power in everyone.
We are the dance of the moon and sun.
We are the hope that will never hide.
We are the turning of the tide.*

—STARHAWK

IF YOU WORK IN A GROUP OF ANY SIZE—SAY, LARGER THAN
about six or eight people—you know that group energy is different than your own energy, and is likely to be different on any given

day or hour on top of that. Working in groups can be incredibly powerful, but it can also be difficult to achieve your goal, or just plain too chaotic to achieve much of anything.

If the group is a tightly knit coven or other very tight magical group, the results can be spectacular and sometimes quite surprising, even for veterans. This type of group energy is so well focused that the sum is truly more than the parts, with all members understanding exactly what is expected of them, when they should act, and what the intended results of this working are supposed to be. Everyone trusts everyone else to carry out their role, so that none of the group's energy is dissipated by missed cues, distractions, or other foul-ups.

The larger the group, the harder it is to organize the workings of the ritual, and the more chaotic the situation can become, due to many factors. This is especially true of groups brought together quickly, rituals with very large crowds in attendance, or people who are not experienced at working with others (especially if they're not even in the same magical tradition). Medium-size public rituals, involving anywhere from fifteen to fifty people, can be done pretty much according to plan, but the HP or HPS should assume that at least one thing will not go the way he or she thought it would. This can be something minor like somebody needing to use the bathroom in the middle of the ritual, something unfortunate and inconvenient like a malfunctioning CD player, or something catastrophic like half the cast not showing up or someone's robes catching fire. Chances are, however, that the medium-size ritual can be saved by some grace and strength, depending on the severity of the disaster.

The large or very large public rituals, however, require multiple clergy members to keep the wilder energies in check and to keep each other stable. These workings, which can be number from fifty people up to more than a thousand in attendance, are pretty much controlled chaos, with the circle needing to be cast very strongly, or the sacred space needing to be heavily grounded, to stop things from going completely haywire. Those running the ritual must be used to working together, preferably members of the same circle/coven/temple/magical group so that they will know how to handle the crowd, take care of each other, handle the energies raised, and not be worrying about what the others are doing.

Large rituals should not try to do too much. Don't try to do a complex energy working with a sizable group of people who don't know each other unless you want a complex mess or a complete flop. It's the old K.I.S.S. rule—Keep It Simple, Stupid! A general "cone of power"–type raising is fine for a large group, especially if it's focused by a spiral dance or something else that the majority of people in attendance will understand. This is the same for all parts of the ritual—the larger the crowd, the more likely there will be a larger number of people who have no idea what you're doing, so if you want audience participation keep it extremely simple and easily explained. The larger the crowd, the simpler the working should be.

When you want order in a ritual, the less audience participation the better in an extremely large group—but don't leave them out completely! Make sure to provide things they can do so that they don't feel like they're watching a stage play: a well-crafted guided meditation; a spiral or other simple dance; a basic procession to, from, around, or through something; some quickly learned songs; and so on. It's the whole reason they came, after all—to participate in their religion.

When you are ready to handle a little more disorder in your rituals in exchange for a more potent result, involve everyone a little more. Selena Fox, HPS of Circle Sanctuary and very experienced in running large group rituals, told me that "I have found that the more interactive a ritual is, the more powerful it is." In addition, she has a number of "housekeeping" tips to not only keep a large ritual under control and running smoothly, but also help everyone present be active participants in the ritual for a more powerful experience for everyone:

> The larger the group, the greater the diversity and the greater the need to have ritual components that work well with that diversity. The larger the numbers, the more a ritual facilitator needs to be concerned about having everyone see, hear, and move together. For very large group rituals, it is important to have a team of assistants to monitor and work with group energy.
>
> Facilitators of large rituals can benefit from having assistants on the periphery of the circle who help in monitoring, and nonverbal signals (such as hand gestures) for communication, such as to increase volume of speaking. Pay attention to facilitators and help them as needed and as appropriate, such as if a ritual facilitator is trying to start a chant to shift the group energy, join in right away, or if there is a signal to start a circular walking movement, start doing this.

Changes should be made as needed to enhance group attunement, attention, and comfort and to keep the ritual in line with its intended purpose. Some examples of changes that I have introduced in the midst of rituals include drawing a group physically closer together to improve cohesion and to aid in hearing and seeing, creating (on-the-spot) and guiding short simple chants to raise energy or tone it down as needed, and having participants sit or stand or change body posture in some way to aid in physical comfort of participants. If some kind of interruption happens in a ritual, the facilitator needs to help the group move on from this.

When asked what common mistakes she's seen ritual facilitators make, Fox replied:

1. Starting a ritual very late, resulting in an impatience/boredom factor among some/all participants and even causing some who had planned to be part to leave.
2. Attempting to do a ritual process (such as full-body individual smudging) that works well in a coven of a dozen or less with a large group, resulting in a long, drawn-out ritual with diminished energy.
3. Not speaking clearly and loud enough for everyone to hear.
4. Being too focused on ritual form and not focused enough on ritual process.
5. Not having enough illumination for nighttime rituals.
6. Not having enough assistants for the size of the group.

In addition to Fox's list, M. Macha NightMare lists these things as common mistakes she's encountered in rituals: "Ego-involvement. Hubris. Overdeveloped sense of self-importance." And it's true, these can be very problematic, especially if any experienced magic workers sense them on the part of the HP/HPS during the ritual and become distracted or irritated. Leaders may think they're the Witch King or Queen and that they can handle a large ritual through their own charisma alone, which can lead to a dissatisfying ritual or even a disaster if knowledgeable people don't step in when there's trouble or aren't involved in the first place.

Aside from the basic practicalities of organizing and herding that many cats . . . er, Pagans, there is the group energy to consider. The Pagan ritual is not a business meeting or a sock hop—it is a method by which everyone helps raise energy for a purpose, and thus the handling of this energy needs special consideration and forethought. Remember, the larger the ritual, the greater the chaos, or—as Macha NightMare sums it up—"The energy of larger groups is much more disparate, more difficult to shape, and fraught with wild cards."

For example, once during a ritual drumming workshop I attended, the instructor explained that whenever there's more than about eight people at a ritual, there's usually a "wobble" in the energy just before it peaks. The more people, the more pronounced the wobble, and the harder it is to keep things going. This funky spot in the energy raising can show up as a brief period where the music kind of falls apart for a second then regroups stronger than before for the release. It can also be felt in other ways if music or

humming is not being used to achieve the traditional cone of power or other forms of energy focusing.

I have definitely found this to be true. I noticed the wobble on my own before it was pointed out, but never really paid much attention to what might be causing it or how it should be worked with. Actually, I don't know what the cause is, and the drumming instructor didn't elaborate. But it's definitely there—see if you notice the wobble at your next large ritual. Perhaps it's coming from the group sensing the energy nearing its peak and getting distracted, or it could be from inexperienced people not understanding when to stop raising energy and ending it prematurely. If you do notice this phenomenon, see whether you can determine its cause.

If you are running the ritual or in charge of leading the music/chants/drumming, the solution to the wobble is simple. As soon as you detect that things are starting to get a little funky, such as a noticeable number of participants no longer singing or drumming or a discernable dip in the energy level, immediately step out to where people can see you and lead them back into the rhythm. Wave your arms as if you're conducting an orchestra that's really far away (if you're not drumming) and sing or drum louder. Make eye contact and make it clear that people should continue to participate, and speed up the tempo to clue them in that the peak has not been reached yet but is nearly there. This should restore the group focus and bring things around to the true peak of the energy and its release.

Part of one Bast ritual I led was an attempt to run various kinds

of energy through drumming and music. When we tried it, however, the "music" was little better than a sort of chaotic noise, with
everyone doing his or her own thing and not really listening to
each other. I mentioned this in a lighthearted way before a second
attempt, and asked everyone to try to come up with a more organized effort the second go-round. The drumming turned out just
like before, with everyone channeling a unique interpretation of
the energy without listening to what the others were doing. I even
tried the trick of standing up and drumming a simple and steady
beat very loudly. A few people did see me stand and try to direct
the group, but the rest weren't having any of it—and we ended up
with chaos a second time.

Sometimes, despite your best effort toward how you want these
things to go, the group energy dictates another path. Sometimes
the best thing is to just let go and allow things to happen as they
will. As long as the results won't be harmful, there's nothing wrong
with a little chaos or an unintended result during a ritual. Sometimes these bits of serendipity allow for new discoveries.

I was at one ritual, however, that allowed chaos energy to go too
far. This was the main Saturday-night ritual of a weekend festival,
and pretty much everyone but the kitchen staff was there. We were
all excited and flush with anticipation, ready for a great ritual with
about three hundred participants. It started off great, with an
honoring of the crones procession, then turned toward the main
part of the ritual.

I honestly don't remember what the intent of the ritual was,
and I felt like I was getting some kind of natural high. My cabinmates and I became really silly and giddy, but another friend of

mine over by the drums looked distinctly unhappy and I couldn't fathom why—I felt terrific and was one of the first to leap up when a spiral dance was started to raise energy. We danced and spun, spiraling around and around, until the energy was raised, then returned to our seats. But my friend near the drums was gone.

The ritual concluded, feeling incomplete somehow, but we were all hungry and ready for dinner in the dining hall. One of our cabinmates said she was going to walk over to the next campground and use the phone, and we waved good-bye. We all felt energetic but strange, as if something in the air wasn't quite right. Our friend didn't show up for dinner. After dinner, she still wasn't in the camp. By 9 P.M. we notified the festival staff that she was missing and sent out a search party. She finally wandered into camp at about 10 P.M., embarrassed and confused.

She explained that she had gone off to use the phone and despite following the road going directly to the other camp, somehow became disoriented and began to wander the forest, feeling somewhat drugged. She stumbled upon the ranger's house and he gave her a ride back to camp, much to everyone's relief.

I saw my other friend the next day—the woman who had left the ritual early. She said that she'd just gotten a Reiki attunement that morning and the chaos energy being run was too much for her. "Didn't you notice?" she said to me. "The spiral dance was going widdershins." I suddenly realized what had happened at the ritual, and why my cabinmate had become disoriented and lost.

To further matters, I found out later that the group running the ritual was a coven of chaos Witches, and part of the reason they wanted to run the main ritual was to use the resulting energy to secretly summon a spirit dragon that would link to everyone present and continue to feed off their energy for the coven's benefit. Needless to say, when this was discovered, all festival attendees were notified and asked to sever this energy link; the chaos Witches were banned from ever attending the annual festival again.

What could have prevented this from happening? Perhaps better energy monitoring during the ritual and better investigation of the group before they were allowed to run it. Can you think of other ways this kind of disaster could have been avoided?

Now it's time for an example of how a perfectly attuned group can truly make magic. One of the most unforgettable experiences I've ever had in a large group ritual was in the late 1980s during the Samhain Spiral Dance ritual put on by Reclaiming Collective. The ritual was broken up into three separate themed nights, Friday night being the more traditional Witch's Samhain, Saturday being the "multicultural ritual," and Sunday being a women's ritual. Each night the San Francisco Women's Building was filled to capacity with about four hundred eager Witches, ready for a ritual.

The ritual began, the ancestors were called, the meditation was deep, and the energy raising began. We danced the spiral dance, of course, but somehow as we whirled faster and faster, it was something like the tigers turning to butter in the famous old folktale. We all became one unit, one body, one energy, and somehow we knew exactly when the energy peaked. As one, we all collapsed to the floor, the chants we had been singing turning into one perfect cosmic "oum." Usually when a large group tries to do a single sound like this, there's dissonance from the chaos energy in the room—and just plain tone-deaf people, too. But this note was perfect.

I swear the auditorium left the earthly plane that night as we all maintained and held that perfect note. There was a golden light filling the room, which became a thicker and thicker mist as the sound continued. I kept trying to blink it away as if my eyes had become cloudy, but the bright golden mist continued to thicken until I could barely make out the other side of the room. Then, as one, we all raised one hand and reached toward the East, saluting the spirits there. The note continued, and again, as if someone was giving us all cues to do so, we swung our hands around to honor the South, then the West, then the North in turn. When we were done and raised our hands to the center, the perfect sound died away gently, the mist disappeared, and the room was left absolutely silent.

Perfection. The One. The Silent Universe. Ma'at.

I haven't seen a ritual like that since, and I doubt I will again. It's a perfect example of a group, even one with better than three hundred people, working together as one unit and letting the energy be what it is without personal egos mucking it up. That's what the divine is—the central spirit who absorbs your ego so that you can become one with the Light when you pass on. Briefly, we were all a part of that group consciousness that night.

I've been to the larger Spiral Dance at the Fort Mason Center in San Francisco since then, trying to recapture that golden light, but haven't found it yet. Perhaps there are too many people (more than twelve hundred attend that one), or perhaps the energy is just too chaotic, or the hall is too large (Fort Mason is a cavernous former warehouse dock), or it's too far away from the earth for good grounding (it's up on piers high over the bay). Whatever the case, it's a very different feeling from the more intimate hall used in years past.

If you are the HP/HPS of a ritual, often you will be expected to channel and/or focus the energy the group has raised and direct it to the goal. As with any energy work, you are merely the hollow conduit; you should not fill yourself up with the extra energy or you risk mental or physical harm, especially if the ritual is a very large one. Feel free to add your own energy to the release if you feel that you've taken in too much, or retain some of the group energy if you feel weak and depleted. Don't be a martyr—take care of yourself so that you're not a wreck when the ritual is over. Concentrate on becoming a hollow tube that merely directs the energy running through it.

Selena Fox had this to say regarding personal energy, group energy, and how the HP/HPS can prepare for a ritual:

> I experience myself being a conduit for the group spirit. My attention is predominantly focused on the group when I am facilitating. Although I continue to be aware of my own personal process as individual that is part of the ritual group, this focus becomes secondary. I put the needs of the group and the ritual experience before my own. My energy shifts to group focus not only immediately before a ritual as part of pre-rite preparations, but I also experience this when doing

ritual design and planning. I stay in group focus mode through-out the ritual as well as in the time following.

If you haven't worked in a group of people before, especially a large group, here is an exercise to help you feel what that energy can be like. Start with a "coven-size" group of people first, then try this with the largest group you can get together. Start by having everyone sit in a circle and hold hands. People can close their eyes or not, as they prefer. Now have everyone run energy between each other, from the person on the right of them, through their body, to the person on the left of them. Start this off gentle and slow at first, then, when everyone's feeling the motion of it, start spinning it a little faster. See what their (and your) reaction is to this. Then get the energy spinning around even faster until it's a blur, then ask the group what they feel. Slow it down gradually, until it finally comes to rest. At the moment the energy stops spinning, have everyone ground it and let people ground and center as needed.

Now try spinning the energy the other way, counterclockwise. See if your reactions or those of the group are different than be-fore. Speed it up, hold it, gather reactions, then ground it as before and let people ground and center as needed. If the group is up for it, have each person spend a moment to call upon her patron/ma-tron deity (assuming she has one...if not, simply use the God or the Goddess) and let her channel a bit of that unique energy. Now repeat the spinning energy, and see if you and the others can tell the difference in this energy.

When you're ready to run a larger ritual, first determine who will be helping you and the level of his experience, especially at running rituals. Remember, the larger the group, the more facilitators you will need, and don't be afraid to ask for help—no one will think less of you and everyone will enjoy the ritual that much more. If you have an enthusiastic helper without much experience, give him one simple task that he can be in charge of and do really well. Every bit of delegation helps, especially when you can trust that the other people will get their bits done right.

You will also need people to monitor the group energy as the ritual progresses in case you are too wrapped up in other functions to monitor it yourself. Once again, the more people, the more potentially chaotic the energy and the more energy monitors you will need. These people will need to be on the sidelines much more, perhaps physically sitting apart from the group and not participating in the ritual to ensure an impartial and levelheaded assessment of the situation if the ritual is very large.

As the HP/HPS, you will be working directly with that group energy and directing it toward the goal. As such, you will need energy handling and control skills to help direct, contain, and even wrangle the group's energy (the latter if it's becoming detrimentally chaotic). Draw upon all your personal ritual experiences, public ritual experiences, and your own "bag of tricks" if need be to help the ritual be a successful and safe one. Some ideas, discussed at length in previous chapters, include using a personal energy matrix to shape and contain energy, color or pattern visualizations, Veilwork, and so on. Every ritual will be different, so be sure you're ready to handle any situation with flexibility and quick-witted actions.

Like everything else in this book (and in magic work in general), it takes skill and experience to handle group energy with proficiency and grace. Don't be put off by the thought of taking the energy of many other people and directing it where it needs to go! Have confidence that with enough exposure to energy-working techniques and enough practice at sensing and handling the collective power of the group at your ritual, you will be able to serve them well and ensure that everything goes off smoothly.

Conclusion

THROUGHOUT THIS BOOK I HAVE BEEN WARNING YOU TO BE EXTREMELY cautious when attempting anything too far outside your own knowledge or abilities. I don't want to throw the baby out with the bathwater, however—this book was written to inspire you, to perhaps open a few doors, to make a few light bulbs appear over some heads.

This book was written for the experienced practitioner, and so perhaps some of this information is nothing new to someone who has "been there done that" in magic circles. The intent was to present a thoughtful and well-balanced view of workings being done across this beautiful Earth, workings to heal, to protect, to change, and to help others.

We are the Priests and Priestesses of magic. Just like skilled physicians, some of us may have innate talents in certain areas and may choose to specialize in them. Like physicians, some of us may be good general practitioners that work well with the overall picture. Some of us may have the desire but not the skill and have to work twice as hard to achieve the sweet rewards of working magic well. The result is what matters—helping others have a better life.

In my Egyptian Temple we understand that we are there for

four purposes: To help ourselves, to help our Temple brethren, to help keep Ma'at (justice; balance; literally, "the way things should be") working in the world, and to honor the Netjeru (all Gods of Egypt). I believe this purpose is the same for any magic worker, for you cannot affect one of these things without affecting the others. Thus, it is in everyone's best interest to have a working understanding, or at least knowledge of, the possibilities that magic gives to us every day. Magic is a tool. You are a tool. When the two are combined with skill and the intent to help others, miracles occur. That is why I wrote this book—what miracles can you create?

We are the children, siblings, lovers, and friends of the Gods. We dance the Spiral Dance of life. We help bring magic and Spirit into the world. We touch the Veil's Edge and, on occasion, see beyond it to discover places of wonder, the land of the Gods.

I rise and walk. The sky arcs ever around; the world spreads itself beneath my feet. We are bound mind to Mind, heart to Heart—no difference rises between the shadow of my footsteps and the will of the Gods. I walk in harmony, Heaven in one hand, Earth in the other. I am the knot where two worlds meet. Red magic courses through me like the blood of Isis, magic of magic, spirit of spirit. I am proof of the power of gods. I am water and dust walking.

—*Awakening Osiris: The Egyptian Book of the Dead,*
translation by Normandi Ellis

Bibliography

Aaland, Mikkel. *Sweat: The Illustrated History of Saunas, Saunas, Roman Baths, and More*, 1997. 27 June 2002, <http://www.cyberbohemia.com/Pages/sweat.htm>.

Briggs, Katharine. *An Encyclopedia of Fairies* (New York: Pantheon Books, 1976).

Broad, William J. "Earth Speaks of the Oracle." *International Herald Tribune* (21 March 2002, Web edition).

Clifton, Chas S. (editor). *Witchcraft and Shamanism* (*Witchcraft Today* series, book three). (St. Paul: Llewellyn Publications, 1994).

Davies, Paul, and John Gribbon. *The Matter Myth* (New York: Simon & Schuster, 1992).

Defenestrate-Bascule, Orryelle. *The Global Chakra Weavings*. June 2002, <http://www.crossroads.wild.net.au/vision.htm>.

Des'tai, Cara, "The Internet Goes Mythic." *Fate* (March 2001).

Dye, Lee, *Colored Worlds*. 28 March 2002, <http://www.abcnews.com>.

Eliade, Mircea. *Shamanism: Archaic Techniques of Ecstasy* (New York: Bolligen Foundation, 1964).

Glossolalia. 9 July 2002, <http://www.bible411.com/glossolalia/>.

Goodman, Felicitas D. *Where the Spirits Ride the Wind* (Bloomington: Indiana University Press, 1990).

Gribbon, John. *In Search of Schrödinger's Cat: Quantum Physics and Reality* (New York: Bantam, 1984).

Herbert, Nick, Ph.D. Interview on *Thinking Allowed* with Dr. Jeffrey Mishlove, 1998.

Ingerman, Sandra. *Medicine for the Earth* (New York: Three Rivers Press, 2000).

Jones, Evan John with Chas. Clifton. *Sacred Mask, Sacred Dance* (St. Paul: Llewellyn Publications, 1997).

Krucoff, Mitchell W., M.D. "Integrative Noetic Therapies as Adjuncts to Percutaneous Intervention During Unstable Coronary Syndromes: Monitoring and Actualization of Noetic Training (MANTRA) Feasibility Pilot." *American Heart Journal* (11 July 2001), pp. 760–7.

Lovelock, James. *The Ages of Gaia* (New York: Norton, 1988).

Marks, Kate. *Circle of Song* (Lenox: Full Circle Press, 1993).

Marton, K. I. "Distant Healing—A Useful Tool?" *Journal Watch* (12 January 1999, Web edition).

Meditation Mapped in Monks. 1 March 2002, <http://news.bbc.co.uk/hi/english/sci/tech/newsid_1847000/1847442.stm>.

Oz. *Between Sanity and Madness*, 25 April 2002, <http://www. chasclifton. com/books/chap2.html>.

Rae, Alastair. *Quantum Physics: Illusion or Reality?* (Cambridge: Cambridge University Press, 1986).

Rause, Vince. "Searching for the Divine." *Reader's Digest* (December 2001).

Rubik, Beverly, Ph.D. Interview on *Thinking Allowed* with Dr. Jeffrey Mishlove, 1998.

Sicher, F., E. Targ, et al. "A Randomized Double-Blind Study of the Effect of Distant Healing in a Population with Advanced AIDS: Report of a Small Scale Study," summary. *Western Journal of Medicine* (December 1998), pp. 356–63.

Stewart, Ian. *Does God Play Dice? The Mathematics of Chaos* (New York: Basil Blackwell, 1989).

Wolf, Fred Alan, Ph.D. Interview on *Thinking Allowed* with Dr. Jeffrey Mishlove, 1998.

Index